# 99% Grace?

# 99% Grace?

HOW FREE IS MAN'S WILL?

Justas Iam

Copyright © 2017 by Justas Iam.

All rights reserved. No part of this publication may be reproduced, distributed or transmitted in any form or by any means, including photocopying, recording, or other electronic or mechanical methods, without the prior written permission of the publisher, except in the case of brief quotations embodied in critical reviews and certain other noncommercial uses permitted by copyright law. For permission requests, write to the publisher, addressed "Attention: Permissions Coordinator," at the address below.

Iam/New Harbor Press
558 E. Castle Pines Pkwy, Ste B4117
Castle Rock, CO 80108
www.netharborpress.com

99% Grace?/ Justas Iam —1st ed.
ISBN 978-1-63357-122-8

Scripture quotations marked "KJV" are taken from the Holy Bible, King James Version (Public Domain). Some portions of the scripture have been underlined and put in bold-face type for emphasis.

The Bondage of The Will, 10th printing. Copyright 1957 by James Clarke & Co. Ltd.; Reprinted by permission of Baker Publishing Group.

Freedom of The Will, 1996 reprint by Soli Deo Gloria. Published in1845 by Thomas Nelson, London; No permission required by fair use tenet per Sean McDonald of Reformation Heritage Books.

Absolute Predestination, 2001 printing by Sovereign Grace Publishers. 2001 copyright by Jay P. Green, Sr.; (public domain book, no permission required).

A Body of Divinity, 2011 reprint by The Banner of Truth Trust. First published in 1692; Reprinted by permission of The Banner of Truth Trust.

The Other Side of Calvinism, 2nd printing 2002, Copyright 1991 by Laurence M. Vance, Vance Publications; Reprinted by permission of Laurence M. Vance

Chosen, But Free, 2nd edition, Copyright 1999,2001 by Bethany House Publishers; Reprinted by permission of Baker Publishing Group.

Beyond Calvinism and Arminianism, 1st edition, Copyright 2002 by C. Gordon Olson; Reprinted by permission of C. Gordon Olson.

Divine Sovereignty, Human Freedom and Responsibility in Prophetic Thought, Printed by Faith Ministries and Publications; Reprinted by permission of Kathy Freeman, Faith Ministries and Publications.

## An independent review of "99% Grace?"
### By Rod Olodeen
### Supervisor, Manuscript Evaluation
### Accurance Publishing Services

99% Grace? is a welcome addition to the new line of promising new works that seek to make religious topics more relevant in today's highly material world. It is thoroughly researched, clearly discussed, adequately argued propositions, sufficiently criticized ideas, leaving almost nothing behind—truly a product of one's life work based on actual experience and labor, without the conventions of formal training. It is indubitably a must-have book for many people, either religious, scholarly, or plain common folks who simply love to read and expand their understanding about things like predestination versus grace, religious beliefs/convictions, limitations of human understanding, etc.

Offering a fresh, novel take on an age-old, but still very interesting and ongoing debate— drawn from almost 40 years of study, contemplation, and development—this book is a sound publishing approach. In today's world of "been there, done that" mentality, an opus such as 99% Grace? offers a much-needed hiatus from the seeming deadlock of the two opposing views on human salvation. Throughout the book, the author aptly gives a number of reasons why his work is out of the ordinary in its genre.

For one, contrary to the long-standing debate between proponents of predestination and of free will, the author did not follow the similar approach typically used by many pastors and scholars who poorly attempted to settle these two paradoxical views by offering a compromised, consenting theology or to simply setting aside the matter by categorizing it as an entirely faith-based concept.

Another critical argument raised by the author highlights the two pivotal errors in reasoning behind the Genesis creation story. First is the fallacy that the free will of man should be considered in the same standing as that of God since the latter was made in the image of God. Second is that man's will has the same level of freedom of Adam and Eve prior to the Great Fall. The author avers that because of these two logical/theological blunders, all resulting arguments that support the preeminence of free will in man's salvation are inevitably bound to also fail.

Another ingenious, perhaps original premise offered by the author is about God's propensity to elect ordinary men and women to write His scriptures—like "David, Amos, Peter and John." The author cleverly applies this to himself, being untrained in formal theology but with abundance in faith, experience, and personal relationship with the Gospel he first met and embraced 39 years ago. The author also attributes some of the flaws that he argues against to the sin of pride which, in most theological debate, often successfully restrains anyone's capacity for objective listening.

After ensuring that both sides of the debate are adequately presented based on fresh or more in-depth and relevant materials—for a more balanced discussion and providing rational explanations—the author can be said to have successfully produced a compelling work for both theological experts and untrained lay people who hunger for Christian truths and the like.

The author's pitch in the book's introduction—that it is not just one of "those" works and the fervent hope that readers will find something "new" in it—epitomize the entirety of 99% Grace? Anyone can also appreciate the clarity and coherence of the discussions as well as how the author's arguments progressed to arrive at his bottom line intent, which is in support of comprehensible and consistent systematic theology on human salvation, or the shift from "Whosoever will" to "Whomsoever I will."

# Contents

Foreword ............................................................................. 1

Introduction ........................................................................ 5

Chapter 1: Doctrinal Rigidity—Perpetual Division ................... 15

Chapter 2: The War Continues: Calvinism versus Arminianism ........................................................................ 21

Chapter 3: A Brief Historical Perspective ................................. 27

Chapter 4: A Critique of Dr. Vance's The Other Side of Calvinism ............................................................................. 53

Chapter 5: The Limits, Implications, and Hearing Ability of Man's Will ........................................................................ 77

Chapter 6: The Will - Free or Not So Free? That Is the Question ................................................................. 91

Chapter 7: Biblical Perspectives about the Will of Man .......... 103

Chapter 8: Assorted Thoughts and Some Views of Others on Free Will ............................................................................. 133

Chapter 9: Election—Why?, Who?, What? and Man's Hatred of It ........................................................................... 147

Chapter 10: Faith - Is It a Gift or a Work? ............................... 165

Chapter 11: God's Sovereignty in Salvation ........................... 181

Chapter 12: Additional Arguments Against Free Will Doctrine .................................................................. 201

Chapter 13: Contexts, New Signage, Food for Thought, Last Words .................................................................. 211

Postscript .................................................................. 221

Appendix .................................................................. 223

Scripture Index .................................................................. 227

# Foreword

IF YOU SUSPECTED THAT the author's name on the cover of this book, Justas Iam, was a pen name, you were correct. You might ask, "Why the pen name?" It is natural for anyone who opens a book on a theological subject like "free will" to inquire about who the author is and what his or her credentials are. Here are my answers to those questions.

I opted for this pen name because I am not a seminary-educated pastor or teacher. I am merely a born-again believer in Jesus Christ whose heart was opened to the gospel forty years ago at the age of thirty-two. As my faith has grown under the effect and influence of many sermons, Sunday school lessons, Bible studies, books by Christian authors, and hours spent personally reading the Bible, the unresolved debate about the first cause of salvation has become a focus of my attention and investigation.

When I set out to write this book, I did not want readers to prematurely weigh the potential worth of its contents against my personal credentials, or lack thereof. I have an ardent desire for coherent theology, but I do not hold any theological degrees. By "coherent theology," I mean a belief system that sits at the highest level of non-contradiction with the sum of the whole council of God—the Bible. The issue of how a man is saved lies at the foundation of all theological debates because salvation is the main theme of Scripture. I am just a lay Christian who desires to express a defense of God's sovereignty in salvation and argue against what I believe to be the false premises of free will doctrine as it relates to salvation. I hope there will be some thoughts and conclusions within this book that the reader has not encountered before.

As I was looking for possible publishers for this book, I was amused by the submission requirements of many of them, which either directly or indirectly stated that they would not consider any theological treatises from anyone who lacked sufficient credentials as a pastor or seminarian. This requirement makes me ask, "Who taught the first seminarian?" It is a good thing that God did not make such a demand of those chosen to write his Scriptures. Moses, David, Amos, Peter, and John, to name just a few, would have been disqualified. God is still able to convey truth through common men, and that is my intention with this book. Is God still able to make a point through a common believer? I hope so.

Granted, there is no shortage of books that address the debate over God's sovereignty in salvation and man's act of belief to gain salvation. As just stated, this is a debate about cause. From my years of studying the Bible and from reading the conclusions of many notable theologians and pastors, I have concluded that this long-running, unresolved debate is the result of a *post hoc, ergo propter hoc* fallacy approach by many theologians. The Latin name for this logical fallacy translates as "after this, therefore because of this." Put in other words, it suggests that "because B follows A, therefore A must be the cause of B." The fallacy lies in concluding that just because one event is said to necessarily follow another event, the first event is conclusively the cause of the second event. In the context of the sovereignty versus free will debate addressed in this book, the presumed first event—willful belief—is scripturally and repeatedly stated as the necessary antecedent of salvation. The Bible is abounding in examples that represent this sequence of these two events. As a result, it is the conclusion of many Christians that such belief is therefore the prime cause of salvation. The fallacy arises from the fact that although belief must precede salvation, it is an error to conclude that man's act of belief itself is the first cause of salvation. It is akin to knocking down a line of five dominoes set up on end by pushing the first domino and then deducing that the action of the fourth domino falling is the only reason the fifth domino fell over. The fourth domino is the immediate cause, but it is not the prime cause. Discovering what ultimately caused the fourth domino to fall would thereby reveal the true cause for why the fifth domino fell. (There are five "dominoes" (events) in the salvation process that will be detailed at the end of Chapter 9.) The focus of this book regards the cause of salvation. Specifically, what is the prime cause? Is it God's sovereign and willful choosing or man's free will believing?

I intend to demonstrate that this seemingly very logical and even easily defended biblical sequence is not as simple as it appears. If one gives it some thought, the question should arise: How and why does saving belief occur? This question will be thoroughly discussed in subsequent chapters. I will attempt to show that the connection between belief and salvation are better described in the context of another Latin expression, *cum hoc, ergo propter hoc*, which translates as "with this, therefore because of this"—the implication being that when two events appear to occur simultaneously or the chronological order of events is uncertain, one event is still defined as the cause of the other. Although cum hoc, ergo propter hoc is still a logical mistake, it does give a truer picture of the relationship between belief and salvation. Any separation of their occurrence is virtually indiscernible. But the deeper question that demands examination still remains: How and why does saving belief occur?

It is hoped that this examination of the question will not result in just another book containing reiterations of past arguments; one that makes no new contribution to the debate on this topic. Instead, it is my hope that the reader might find some thoughts, insights, and perspectives they had not previously considered. I admit, at the outset, to a firm belief that every individual's salvation is a sovereign, predestined work of God. Whether you agree or disagree with how I use various biblical verses to defend my position, I ask for your indulgence in considering the insights and explanations that are put forth. Regardless of your present view of the matter, reading this work may either reinforce your current position or, perhaps, may change your thinking about this most important doctrinal question.

If it is agreed that there are only two feasible views on this doctrinal issue and only one can be correct, then it becomes appropriate for all Christians to seek the truth of the matter. This is an issue on which every believer, consciously or subconsciously, must stand on one side or the other. The Holy Spirit will—no, must—guide anyone who honestly seeks the truth about how and why God chose and saved anyone. Therefore, my real name, as the author, is unimportant. It is my dividing of God's Word and my conclusions that the reader must judge. I hope the sum of the points I offer are helpful to that end. This is my scriptural motivation for writing this book:

> 1 Pet. 3:15 But sanctify the Lord God in your hearts: and <u>be ready always to give an answer</u> to every man that asketh you a reason of the hope that is in you with meekness and fear.

My answer is this: I believe that salvation is 100 percent the work of the grace of God, not 99 percent. My salvation and my hope rest on God's grace alone.

# Introduction

MR. AND MRS. ADAM and Eve stepped through the gate of their former estate, the Garden of Eden. As God shut the gate and it locked behind them and they started down the path ahead, Adam stopped.

"What's wrong?" Eve asked.

"Something is different," Adam replied.

Eve answered incredulously, "Are you kidding? Just look at the path ahead of us compared to the garden we have just being evicted from."

Adam ignored her sarcasm. "No, it's more than that. It is a strange feeling inside. Back there it felt peaceful being in God's presence. He told us what to do and not to do. Now we are alone and must decide for ourselves what to do and how to live."

Eve thought for a moment. "There's nothing we can do about it. Let's go."

"Okay, but something is definitely different inside us. Don't you feel it?"

"Yes, I think I do, but for now we are free to do whatever we want to. We can do this, can't we?"

Still pondering the situation, Adam continued, "I guess we can, but what about our descendants? We have lost access to eternal life through the Tree of Life, and we know we can't go back to it. What if our descendants believe that they are able to use their own wills to choose and recover the eternal life that we lost in the Garden?"

"Well can't we just tell them the problem?"

"We can, but they won't believe us. Our only access to eternal life is out of reach."

Eve worried, "Oh my, then how will we, and our descendants, ever recover our position as God's children?"

"Remember when God told us what our burdens would be when we left the Garden because of our sin? Remember also what He told Satan? God told him, 'I will put enmity between you and the woman and between your seed and her seed.'"

"Yes, I remember."

Adam continued, "God also told Satan that the woman's seed shall bruise his head and then he shall bruise the heel of the seed of the woman."

"I remember, but what does it mean?"

"I'm not sure, but it sounds like God will somehow save us and our descendants in the future. Our obedience failed in the garden, but we must go on from here and try to obey God. We must trust Him to show us when and how He will save us," Adam said.

Thus began the odyssey of all mankind into their captivity of sin. Their relationship with their creator was severed. They were now left to navigate life as their own gods.

In this hypothetical discussion, Adam and Eve quite possibly would have felt an internal difference because they had personally experienced a change in their natures. They were transformed from having no inclination to sin to having a sinful nature that directed their own wills—wills by which they made their own decisions about right and wrong. The difference would have been real for them, but not so for their descendants. We do not sense any difference at all because we are born with and experience only one nature—a fallen one, a god-self one, which we acquired in Adam and Eve. From our birth, we, by nature, do whatever our fallen flesh desires most.

It is a profound truth that most of Adam and Eve's descendants have failed to realize. In the Garden, humans were created with a truly free will. They were friends of God and had no inclination to sin. Once outside the Garden, and ever since, mankind continues to believe that they have a free will simply because they are able to make their own choices. They fail to understand how their nature drives their choices. They fail to believe what the Bible says about the nature of lost man. They cannot see the invisible chains of Satan that hold them in rebellion against God and in allegiance to their new "god-self" nature. Thus, to every descendant of Adam and Eve, the common perception is that they have a "free will."

Moving now from this hypothetical conversation outside Eden to a biblical truth, Adam and Eve also knew that God had hinted at a future salvation from the enemy (Satan), who had deceived them into sin. Today, we don't have to rely on a hinted salvation. God's final salvation instructions to men have been delivered. The Bible tells us all we need to know to become a child of God again. Nevertheless, there is a serious question that remains hanging in the balance within Christianity. It asks, in regard to the choice to believe and be saved, what is the first cause of this choice? Is it God's will or man's will? Lost men care nothing about this question, but within Christianity, this remains a very divisive question. It is a question that challenges the level of God's sovereignty in this most important of all His miracles. It is a question that can only have one correct answer.

If you are a born-again believer in Jesus Christ, how do you answer this question? Between God and yourself, whose choosing is the first step of salvation? This question goes on unresolved as Christian doctrine marches a split path, resolutely committed to either God's total sovereignty in salvation or to the necessity of man's free will choice in the salvation process. These are two realities in the Bible that appear to oppose each other. The Bible tells us about both God's choosing of men to salvation, as well as the fact that men are repeatedly implored to choose to believe the gospel for salvation. Scripture also exhorts us to "rightly divide" the Word of God (2 Tim. 2:15), yet Christianity is far from any unified understanding and agreement about this age-old question. The default response of much of Christendom is to accept the supposed contradiction of these two biblical truths as an unknowable matter that must be relegated to the "by faith only" pigeonhole of one's theology. This need not happen if we would listen more closely to Scripture and let God be God.

Both God and man do make a choice in the miracle of salvation. These are two distinct "choosings" that the Bible reveals to us, but simple logic says that they cannot both be "first." There is a definite cause and effect relationship between them. The truth of what supposed free will really did for man will be examined in depth later in this book. For now, I suggest that determining the correct order of these choices of God's will and man's will is foundational to building a sound system of theology and to a "right dividing" of Scripture. Conversely, believing in the incorrect sequence of these two choices produces a limited view of God, and it diminishes the scope of His grace.

You may wonder what possessed me to tackle such a historically unresolved topic as the first cause of a man's salvation. As I grew in my spiritual maturity as a Christian, the continued conflict within Christianity over this issue intrigued me because of the logical contradiction posed by the two views. I would hear or read persuasive teachings on both sides of the argument. I wrestled with the Scriptures cited by the advocates of both views. Once I became settled on the side of God's total sovereignty in salvation, I found myself constantly alert to teachings

## INTRODUCTION

that seemed to favor man's free will in the matter. Whenever I heard or read any passionate argument for the free will view of salvation, I would be instinctively motivated to find the flaw(s) in either their reasoning or their use of Scripture to justify their view.

My final motivation to write this extensive defense of predestinated salvation came from a weekly small group Bible study that my wife and I lead in our home. We had recently undertaken a study of the very doctrinal book of Ephesians. Of course, if you are familiar with that book at all, you know that in chapter one, verses four and five, the apostle Paul quickly introduces one of the most, if not the most, controversial theological subjects in all of Scripture—predestination. Paul reveals this truth as it was received by him from our ascended and glorified Savior, Jesus Christ. (See Eph. 1:9) Discussions about predestination and election in Ephesians are unavoidable, as shown by the underlined phrases below that Paul uses early in his letter to the church at Ephesus:

> Eph. 1:4 According <u>as he hath chosen us in</u> him before the foundation of the world, that we should be holy and without blame before him in love.

> Eph. 1:5 <u>Having predestinated us unto the adoption of children</u> by Jesus Christ to himself, according to the good pleasure of his will.

> Eph. 1:11 In whom also we have obtained an inheritance, <u>being predestinated according to the purpose of him who worketh all things after the counsel of his own will</u>.

These verses have been among the primary battleground passages on the subject of predestination among Christian theologians, preachers, teachers, and laymen for centuries, stretching back to Augustine. The essential predestination question is: Do men believe the gospel because they are the elect of God or are men the elect of God because they believe the gospel? It is a genuine cause and effect debate. When the predestination issue arose in our study group, a lively discussion ensued.

My wife and I are firm believers of God's total sovereignty in the salvation of any man. The majority of our Bible study group, however, holds to the free-will-of-man side of the question regarding how anyone is saved. Les Feldick Ministries, the producer of the Bible study we were using, is also committed to the belief in the role of free will in the salvation decision. I was aware of the group's position before we arrived at the verses listed above, so the debate was not unexpected. We had our discussion and debate about the predestination issue forcefully yet peacefully.

While no personal positions were changed in our discussions, it was a comment by one gentleman in our group, who took the strongest stand for the free will of man, that caught my attention. He opined that predestination is one of those subjects that is beyond our understanding. He concluded, therefore, that we must be resigned to just accept the doctrine of predestination by faith as an unexplainable truth. Sadly, this is a widely held conclusion in Christendom. It suggests that both truths, predestination and free will, in the context of salvation, are equally and Biblically true. So any supposed contradiction is incomprehensible. I yielded to his view for the moment only because I could see that the group debate was played out and that no one was changing their view.

Predestination is a difficult issue to resolve in open discussion. This is a debate that is more effective when it is presented in an orderly and logical sequence using pertinent verses to support the defense of one's position. It has been my experience that a group debate setting is not conducive to achieving persuasion from either point of view, because the debaters on either side are often too entrenched in their understanding of the issue. In face-to-face theological debate, pride usually suppresses objective listening.

The existence of the Trinity and the simultaneous deity and humanity of Christ are examples of Bible truths which, indeed, must be accepted by faith alone, because they both exceed the capabilities of total human comprehension. However, I do not accept the same conclusion about God's predestination of men. I do not believe it is beyond the grasp of our understanding or that it must be merely relegated to our acceptance by faith. The act of predestination is not a mystery. God has plainly told us that He did some choosing before the beginning of time. While believers must certainly accept this statement of fact by faith, the very act itself, of God making choices, is not beyond our understanding. Although the truths about the Trinity, Christ's simultaneous deity and humanity, and even the creation account in Genesis are beyond our understanding, God's decision-making about salvation is a work we can comprehend. Therefore, the equating of predestination with other incomprehensible truths of God is in error. Why God chose as he did is another matter which will be addressed later.

The major premise of this book is that because the doctrinal propositions of the sovereignty of God in salvation and the free will act of man in salvation are logically antithetical, the correct understanding must be established. Any attempt to place these two biblical truths on an equal footing as prime causes of salvation diminishes our understanding of God's perfect, confusion-free order.

> 1 Cor. 14:33 For God is not the author of confusion, but of peace, as in all churches of the saints.

Consistent, systematic theology cannot contain blatantly contradictory doctrines. Conflicting doctrines, no matter how well Scripture is used to justify them, must be studied and exposed. No amount of faith or theological accommodation can bring these two views of salvation to a state of peaceful coexistence as equal causes of salvation. By definition, in all of creation there can be only one prime cause. A prime cause cannot have any dependency upon any other cause. If it did, it would cease to be the prime cause. God must be sovereign in everything, including the miracle of salvation. Maintaining a view that supposes any dependency upon the role of man's will in salvation requires that some creative, interpretative spin be applied to redirect any Bible verses that seem to support the sovereignty of God view. I postulate that there can be no doctrinal fence-sitting between these two views. The fence between these views is like a knife's edge that maintains a clean divide. A person cannot plant his feet on both sides of the issue and still maintain a coherent theology. The biblical truth of the matter must be sought.

There are many pastors who try, in vain, to reconcile these two doctrines into a non-contradictory theology. Others choose to either ignore the topic of predestination or dismiss it as a "by faith" topic. I have often heard pastors bypass any in-depth exposition of the issue by merely jumping to a simple illustration that excuses them from any further need to try to explain this theological mystery. To resolve the contradiction, the following hypothetical is commonly offered. Pastors ask their audience to imagine a picture of the gateway into heaven. They then proceed to describe it as having two signs, one outside and one inside of the gateway to heaven. The sign on the outside of the gate is inscribed with the well-known thought from John 3:16, which reads, "Whosoever believeth," while the sign on the inside of the gate is drawn from Eph. 1:4, with the phrase, "Chosen us in Him before the foundation of the world." The implication of these two inscriptions creates a contradiction because it suggests that this gate has two keys that allow admittance. The outer sign credits man's will, while the inner sign credits God's will for any passage through this gate. By use of this illustration, many pastors use the contradictory signage on each side of the entrance

## INTRODUCTION

to stand as a representation of an incomprehensible mystery of Scripture. It becomes a clever picture of heaven's entrance that is portrayed as an unresolvable truth, even though there is no such picture given in the Bible. However, for many pastors, this simple picture lets them off the hook, and it puts a convenient end to the requirement of any further explanation. I'll offer a remodeling of this hypothetical gate in Chapter 13 that is more biblically sustainable.

I do not yield to my Bible study friend's suggestion that the issue of predestination be categorized as just another incomprehensible but true Bible mystery. This was the event that prompted me to set out this defense of why I believe that God really does everything according to "the counsel of His own will," (Eph. 1:11) including the foreordained salvation of some, but not all, men. I was not offended by my friend's statement. It was not that I had not heard this opinion before. I believe I understand why people hold this view, however it is a view that is built upon misapplied human logic and experience.

This book is my defense of why I believe that the sum of Scripture tells us that salvation is the sole prerogative and work of the creator God, who alone is the determiner of whom He will save and whom He will pass over. I don't believe that the Lord intended for the truth about how salvation is accomplished to remain a mystery or a contradiction. I do believe the Scriptures provide a non-contradictory, biblical answer to the question. Being chosen for salvation does not afford anyone a reason for pride or boasting. Once a person is saved, the only remaining theological questions are, "how and why did God choose to save me?" The only answer to both questions are, by the grace of God—100 percent grace. All glory accrues to Him.

CHAPTER 1

# Doctrinal Rigidity Perpetual Division

**Rigidity**

I HAVE TWO PRINCIPLE frustrations over this doctrinal stand-off. My first frustration, as mentioned earlier, is with the experienced futility of personal debate. Whenever I engage in any friendly, face-to-face debate on this subject with another believer with the opposite viewpoint, the debate almost inevitably hits an impasse. Personal reasoning and pride kick in, and whatever arguments I try to propose get stalled. My opponents often just stop listening. I am not saying that I don't also use reasoning, or that I am immune to moments of pride. God gave us the gift of logic, and He expects us to use it. Human reason also factors into everyone's biblical interpretations, for better or worse. However, God offers a word of caution through the prophet Isaiah to men seeking to understand Him in an important principle:

> Isa 55:8 For my thoughts are not your thoughts, neither are your ways my ways, saith the Lord.

> Isa 55:9 For as the heavens are higher than the earth, so are my ways higher than your ways, and my thoughts than your thoughts.

This passage should be a warning to us when Scripture runs counter to our logic. When finite men read and interpret the words of an infinite God, it is easy for them overstep their bounds and impose their finite powers of logic upon God and His truth. Christians can easily impose their humanity upon God when they force meanings from His Word that they desire. God reproves this kind of error in the Psalms:

> Ps. 50:21 These things hast thou done, and I kept silence; <u>thou thoughtest that I was altogether such an one as thyself</u>: but I will reprove thee, and set them in order before thine eyes.

In the debate over how God saves anyone, pride often tends to blind people's eyes and deafen their ears whenever they are confronted with the possibility that their theology may be in error. It is curious how quickly the cement of the one's particular theology hardens their willingness to consider the possibility of a new Bible truth that is, in any degree, contradictory to what they believe. This kind of hardening too often shuts down any receptiveness to learning something new. The need for all believers to be Bereans never ceases (Acts 17:10–11). We must always test everything we have been taught on a particular subject with what the Bible says about it, wherever the subject arises in Scripture. Doctrinal rigidity is a positive trait when it comes to standing against the tide of doctrinal erosion that plagues Christianity today. Nevertheless, because Christianity is also polluted with distorted doctrines, doctrinal rigidity is often the very impediment to doctrinal growth and maturity. The apostle John exhorts us, in a way, to guard against such rigidity:

## DOCTRINAL RIGIDITY PERPETUAL DIVISION

> 1 John 4:1 Beloved, believe not every spirit, but <u>try the spirits whether they are of God</u>: because many false prophets are gone out into the world.

It is deceiving spirits who persist in injecting small amounts of leaven (doctrinal distortion) into the lump of Christianity (proper biblical doctrine). Christian denominations, as well as local independent churches, often originate and evolve around erroneous biblical interpretations that men have extracted from Scripture. John also tells where our infallible help comes from when we search for a truth in Scripture:

> John 16:13 Howbeit <u>when he, the Spirit of truth, is come, he will guide you into **all** truth</u>: for he shall not speak of himself; but whatsoever he shall hear, that shall he speak: and he will shew you things to come.

(Notice how much truth He will guide us into if we let Him.)

Thus, both sound and unsound doctrine can become foundations of these various assemblies of believers when they allow their logic to prevail over a Spirit-revealed truth. But men and their organizations remain finite and fallible, so the spirit of the Bereans must be continually employed by all believers. The Spirit will not endorse two contradictory doctrines. One of the best metrics of correct doctrine is the absence of any clear contradictory Scripture. Nevertheless, the negative aspect of doctrinal rigidity is a real problem within Christianity.

### Division

The second and more crucial aspect of my frustration is one which is increasingly perplexing. It is the question of why these two antithetical views have endured so long and have so successfully divided Christians for centuries. The fallback opinion says that these two biblical facts, God's choosing to salvation as opposed to man's free will choosing, are beyond our understanding. This is a cop-out to searching for the correct answer, as the way of God's logic demands. How does His logic demand an answer? If the verse below, from the inerrant Word of God, is true, then God would not provide Scriptures that produce clear, antithetical doctrines. Seemingly scriptural antithesis must be resolved through contextual application, which in turn requires the knowledge of God's progressive dispensational relationship with men.

> 1 Cor. 14:33 <u>For God is not the author of confusion</u>, but of peace, as in all churches of the saints.

For example, the dietary laws given to Israel are not required for obedience by Christians today under the dispensation of grace. Yet many Christians and Christian assemblies in this age still feel bound to apply various degrees of law keeping that were only required of Israel under the law. Paul hammered the point of our not being under law, but under God's grace. It is disappointing and sad that such an answer to this debate has failed to emerge from centuries of Christian scholarship. We can't blame God.

Blatant antithetical doctrine should not be tolerated within the body of Christ, which is the Church. Mysteries of Scripture, such as the Trinity and the deity and humanity of Jesus, must be acknowledged as mysteries of God (Deut. 29:29) and accepted by faith because they are beyond our total comprehension. A mystery is not the same thing as a contradiction (or antithesis). Antithetical doctrine does not belong in the same category as a mystery.

There is little doctrinal peace among the multitude of churches today, even among those that can be legitimately called Christian. I am not naïve as to the ultimate answer regarding why a resolution has evaded Christians for so long. It is, of course, the reality of Satan and his unceasing distortion of God's Word. I understand that Satan is the ultimate source of this confusion among believers. He never ceases to ply men with his lie that repeatedly says, "God did not really say (or mean) this or that" (Gen. 3:5). Nevertheless, logic (of man or of God) says that one of these views of the issue under consideration has to be in error. It is a sad fact that an irrefutable, biblical solution to this error has not been produced by the pens and pulpits of past theologians. Such a response would have effectively exposed what, in my view, is the fallacy of the doctrine of free will. God did not purposefully leave us in a fog about this. I believe the answer is available within the whole counsel of God.

Maybe something in the following chapters will assist the reader in untying this "Gordian knot" of all doctrinal disputes. Rather than dismiss this "knot" as incomprehensible, let's use the combination of Scripture, logic, the biblical evidences of God's attributes of sovereignty, grace, love, and the guidance of the Holy Spirit to lead us to the correct answer of why and how anyone is saved.

CHAPTER 2

# The War Continues: Calvinism versus Arminianism

BOTH SIDES OF THIS historical war over predestination confidently employ Scriptures to demonstrate the authority of their view of this issue. Using their respective arsenals, the attacks, the defenses, and the counter-attacks have continued to this day between two theological views commonly labeled, Calvinism and Arminianism.

If God's Word is the proper boundary within which this doctrinal war is to be fairly waged, and God is not "the author of confusion," then why have Christians through the ages been unable to sort this war out? As previously cited, I see two possible reasons. The first is Satan's unrelenting effort to distort God's Word. Satan's perpetual foundational lie remains, "God did not really say (mean) that," to which men too easily succumb. While God neither slumbers nor sleeps (Ps. 121:4), neither does Satan. This success of Satan's lie, in turn, often seduces men to "wrest" (spin) assorted passages to fit their theology. The second reason, is the pride of men that arises in this debate. Once they affix themselves to a doctrinal premise on one side or the other of an argument, they often become unyielding to any scriptural evidence to the contrary. Pride not only goes before destruction (Prov. 16:18), but it also goes before most all doctrinal stubbornness. No man is immune to it.

Adam and Eve were unaware that when they yielded to Satan's temptation to disobey God's command, they had enlisted on Satan's side of his war against God. War has been an affliction of man ever since Cain turned against Abel regarding the proper sacrifice to offer to God. Wars come in many different contexts. The worst of those contexts are the wars among men over God's word. Nevertheless, wars in a sinful world are inevitable. We know that all Scripture is God-breathed, as 2 Tim. 3:16 says:

> 2 Tim. 3:16 <u>All scripture is given by inspiration of God</u>, and is profitable for doctrine, for reproof, for correction, for instruction in righteousness.

Likewise, we are told in Acts 23 that even the scribes of the Pharisees knew that it was ill-advised to fight against any Word from God:

> Acts 23:9 And there arose a great cry: and the scribes that were of the Pharisees' part arose, and strove, saying, We find no evil in this man: <u>but if a spirit or an angel hath spoken to him, let us not fight against God</u>.

From these two verses it can only be concluded that any doctrine that is in open conflict (war) with some part of Scripture is a war that is also ill-advised. Wars are sometimes necessary to defend rights or correct the wrongs that people commit, but it should be remembered that war is the result of sin, as we are told by the apostle James:

> James. 4:1 <u>From whence come wars</u> and fightings among you? <u>come they not hence, even of your lusts that war in your members</u>? (Here, if James would have had a copy of Paul's letter to the Romans, he could have used Rom. 7:7–11 and 21–23. Paul knew about this war within the individual.)

> James 4:2 Ye lust, and have not: ye kill, and desire to have, and cannot obtain: <u>ye fight and war, yet ye have not, because ye ask not</u>. (What believers often fail to ask for is the guidance of the Holy Spirit to resolve any doctrinal conflicts.)

An indication that one is on the wrong side of the debate is the need to either bend Scripture to accommodate a doctrine or to consciously avoid any troublesome passages. Men should restrain their logic from forced interpretations of God's Word. This is to say that where Bible passages seem to run counter to man's logic, logic should yield to faith over what logic seems to see, or fails to see, thereby letting God be God in his decree of salvation for His elect. It is better for a man to admit to a lack of understanding and seek it from God's Word rather than bend Scripture to fit his own understanding or to fit it into whatever some denominational system of men has told him. Forced outcomes are detrimental in jigsaw puzzles, crossword puzzles, and expository Bible study. Proverbs tells us this very truth:

> Prov. 3:5 Trust in the Lord with all thine heart; and <u>lean not unto thine own understanding</u>.

God's predestining of men to salvation is one such truth that must not be forced to accommodate man's personal logic system. In regard to this issue, Paul wrote in Romans 9 that man does not have the privilege of questioning God about the mysterious topic of His distribution of mercy or hardening.

> Rom. 9:18 Therefore hath he mercy on whom he will have mercy, and whom he will he hardeneth.

Rom. 9:19 Thou wilt say then unto me, Why doth he yet find fault? For who hath resisted his will?

Rom. 9:20 Nay but, <u>O man, who art thou that repliest against God? Shall the thing formed say to him that formed it, Why hast thou made me thus</u>?

As I look at both sides of the sovereignty versus free will debate, it strikes me that the free will position is, in large part, driven by logic and beset by false premises, some of which are derived from personal experience. In contrast, the sovereignty of God position rests upon, and requires, greater faith in who God is and what His Word says, whether one's logic can grasp it or not. Where human logic and required faith clash in a matter of Scripture, man's logic must yield to faith. However, in this doctrinal struggle, I believe Scripture gives us enough information to reveal the grace that God bestows on man by His sovereign election of some men to salvation according to nothing other than His sovereign purpose. The view of men that attributes a necessity of their cooperative free will in salvation is an insult to the totality of God's grace and love.

It was God's choice to reveal the facts of His sovereign election and predestination of men, although He waited to do so through the apostle Paul. Since He is not the author of confusion, it can be said that God did not intend a war to exist among men over predestination. If men would prayerfully and thoughtfully examine the history of the debate and let the Scriptures say what they say, then this particular "war" could be and should be settled. Blatant doctrinal contradictions must be resolved by the whole counsel of God's Word because He is not the author of confusion.

So, will this seemingly endless war among Christians over predestination and free will ever end? Is it possible for it to end? It would be theoretically possible if men would humble themselves before any biblical truth that may strain their human logic. Today, many war-weary non-Christians and even many Christians often plead, "Why can't we just love each other?" Unfortunately, the answer is that among sinful mankind, self-love usually eclipses any degree of love shown to others. War is one of the ongoing evidences of man's fallen condition, especially as they persist in "being their own gods" and pursuing their own interests. Only at the end of Christ's millennial kingdom on earth, when the devil, the beast, the false prophet, and all unbelievers are cast into the lake of fire, will there be an end to all wars. Then God's love will be implanted into all saved men, and it will prevail.

It is usually helpful to understand what various wars are about by studying the historical context in which they evolved. This is what the next chapter will attempt to provide.

CHAPTER 3

# A Brief Historical Perspective

THERE IS A LONG history behind the battle that surrounds the issue of whether God is the sovereign source and cause of anyone's salvation or if salvation is a cooperative result of God's sovereignty and man's free will decision. Since this doctrinal struggle has such a lengthy past, it is beneficial to the reader to become acquainted, or reacquainted, with the history of this debate if they are unfamiliar with it. It should be no surprise that most of the doctrinal disunity that exists today arose from careless dividing of Scripture in Christianity's past. All Christians are liable to incur individual shame from careless dividing, as warned about in 2 Tim. 2:15:

> 2 Tim. 2:15 Study to shew thyself approved unto God, a workman that needeth <u>not to be ashamed</u>, rightly dividing the word of truth.

## Calvinism versus Arminianism

As this doctrinal struggle evolved through the years, its adherents became respectively labeled as either Calvinists or Arminians, depending on which side of the issue they stood. The names attached to each side are derived from a particular era in the history of the dispute, when two theologians became embroiled in the matter at the dawn of the reformation. They are John Calvin, who championed the sovereignty view and Jacobus Arminius, who advocated for the free will of man in the salvation decision. Regrettably, these labels are not universally understood by all Christians, so their attachment is not readily appreciated by those who are so labeled. I recently had a fellow believer, who manages a Christian website, caution me to avoid the use of these labels connected to these two theologians because of the unfortunate connotations they sometimes convey. He recommended that I stick to biblical labeling when discussing this issue. This sounds like a simple solution, but there are no simple biblical labels for the two sides. I will, in the remainder of this defense, at times use the terms Calvinism or Arminianism. But when they appear, their respective meanings are limited to either the view that God is the sovereign determiner of every salvation (Calvinism) or that man's free will has a causative role in the salvation decision (Arminianism). It is only in that context that I will employ these two labels.

**Calvinism Proponents: Sample Views from Four Reformers**

On the proponent side of the sovereignty of God in salvation, I call the reader's attention to the four reformed or Calvinist authors whose books I have read. These men present some of the best defenses of God's sovereign work of salvation. The first book I read was Martin Luther's solid rebuttal to the staunch Arminian, Erasmus, titled, *The Bondage of the Will*. The second was Jonathan Edwards' book, titled, *The Freedom of the Will*. Both of these works, with seemingly contrasting titles, make the same essential conclusions about the operation of man's will. Next, was Jerome Zanchius' most notable work, titled, *Absolute Predestination*. The final reformer I share with the reader, Thomas Watson, delivered a series of sermons on the Westminster Catechism that were later compiled into a book titled *A Body of Divinity*, which was published just a few years after Watson's death.

## Martin Luther (1483–1546)

While he was a Catholic priest, Luther's well-known break from his Catholicism came from God's illumination to him during his study of the book of Romans. It was in this study that the doctrine of "justification by faith" took hold in his understanding of how men were saved. The culmination of his breakaway came when Luther posted his Ninety-Five Theses in Whittenberg, Germany in October 1517. His new view on justification by faith alone was one of the sparks of the Reformation because it stood in direct contradiction to the Roman Catholic doctrine. In response to Luther's doctrinal rebellion, the church issued some decrees about justification at the Council of Trent (1545–1563), which began one year before Luther's death. These decrees were precise declarations of Roman Catholic doctrine, which dominated Christendom at this time in history. Within this lengthy declaration were decrees that defined their view of the place man's will must have in his obtaining of salvation. Later in this book I will be critiquing a book titled *The Other Side of Calvinism* by Dr. Laurence Vance. In his book, Dr. Vance states that in the Council of Trent's decrees on justification, man's will is made central in his justification. Here are two Canons issued by the Council of Trent that represent their view about man's will and Justification:

> Canon 4. If any one saith, that man's free will moved and excited by God, by assenting to God exciting and calling, nowise co-operates towards disposing and preparing itself for obtaining the grace of Justification; that it cannot refuse its consent,

if it would, but that, as something inanimate, it does nothing whatever and is merely passive; let him be anathema.

Canon 9. If any one saith, that by faith alone the impious is justified; in such wise as to mean, that nothing else is required to co-operate in order to the obtaining the grace of Justification, and that it is not in any way necessary, that he be prepared and disposed by the movement of his own will; let him be anathema.[1]

With his new understanding of how God justifies, Luther became a fervent preacher and author in opposition to Arminianism, which was the prevailing doctrine in Catholic theology. He put the gift of salvation back into the sovereign domain of God and removed any cooperative role of man in the process. Nevertheless, it is equally interesting and yet sad that Luther, despite this thunderbolt of revelation from the book of Romans, never relinquished many other works tenets of his Roman Catholic heritage.

Another related and misunderstood Bible truth is the meaning of the Godhead's decision to create man "in our image." (This "image" problem will be discussed further in Chapter 6.) Luther, writing in *The Bondage of the Will*, expounded on the captivity of man's will to his moral nature—his fallen moral nature. Man's fallen moral nature, which was the result of his act of disobedience, altered his God-created free will nature. Unfortunately, this moral nature cannot now be changed back to the original God-created image by man's own will. Man's will is now a captive to his fallen nature and to the power of the god of this world, Satan. A captive cannot, by a mere act of his free will, decide to walk out of his imprisonment. If he can, then he is not truly a captive.

---

[1] "Council of Trent." *Theopedia*. https://www.theopedia.com/council-of-trent.

## A BRIEF HISTORICAL PERSPECTIVE

The following verses legitimately apply to all of Adam's posterity, who are considered to be "in the flesh." While in the immediate context these verses may be addressed to certain groups of people, in the wider context of the words and phrases that are highlighted in bold print, these verses apply to every unsaved man. Listen to how lost men, who are separated from God and under Satan's dominion, are described:

> Gen. 6:5 And God saw that the **wickedness of man was great in the earth**, and that every imagination of **the thoughts of his heart was only evil continually.**

> Rom. 5:10 For if, when **we were enemies**, we were reconciled to God by the death of his Son, much more, being reconciled, we shall be saved by his life.

> Col. 1:21 And you, that were sometime **alienated and enemies in your mind by wicked works**, yet now hath he reconciled.

> Phil. 3:18 (For many walk, of whom I have told you often, and now tell you even weeping, that they are the **enemies of the cross of Christ.**):

> James 4:4 Ye adulterers and adulteresses, know ye not that the friendship of the world is enmity with God? **Whosoever therefore will be a friend of the world is the enemy of God.**

> 2 Cor. 4:4 In whom **the god of this world hath blinded the minds of them which believe not**, lest the light of the glorious gospel of Christ, who is the image of God, should shine unto them.

> John 15:23 **He that hateth me hateth my Father also.**

Luke 19:14 But **his citizens hated him**, and sent a message after him, saying, We will not have this man to reign over us.

Rom. 2:14 For when **the Gentiles, which have not the law, do by nature the things contained in the law, these, having not the law, are a law unto themselves.**

John 8:44 **Ye are of your father the devil**, and the lusts of your father ye will do. He was a murderer from the beginning, and abode not in the truth, because there is no truth in him. When he speaketh a lie, he speaketh of his own: for he is a liar, and the father of it.

Rom. 9:8 That is, They which are the **children of the flesh, these are not the children of God**: but the children of the promise are counted for the seed.

Eph. 2:2 Wherein in time past **ye walked according to the course of this world, according to the prince of the power of the air**, the spirit that now worketh in the children of disobedience.

Eph. 2:3 Among whom also **we all had our conversation in times past in the lusts of our flesh, fulfilling the desires of the flesh and of the mind; and were by nature the children of wrath, even as others.**

These verses do not paint a flattering picture of how God sees "lost" mankind.

We know that these terms do not describe the man Adam, as he was created by Jesus (God). These verses suggest that man's nature underwent a profound change from how God had created him. There is also no suggestion in them that man wants to, nor is able to, by his own volition, believe the offer of salvation that God has revealed to him and thereby escape his captivity to Satan. The last verse noted, Eph. 2:3, confirms this profound change as it precisely describes the plight of all men as being "by nature the children of wrath." Why can these descriptions be legitimately applied to all men? Paul gives us the answer in 1 Corinthians 15 and Romans 6.

> I Cor. 15:22 For as <u>in Adam all die</u>, even so in Christ shall all be made alive.

This verse tells us that "all die." We also know from Romans 6 what the God ordained reason for death is:

> Rom. 6:23 For <u>the wages of sin is death</u>; but the gift of God is eternal life through Jesus Christ our Lord.

Free will advocates love to undermine the doctrine of predestination with the charge that predestination nullifies any responsibility of man for his belief or unbelief of the gospel. They reason that if man's responsibility is voided by God's predestinating work, then man's accountability for any sin is also voided. The doctrine of God's electing of men will be discussed later. For now, I would ask free will proponents this: Why it is fair for "all" to die in Adam, if they had no part in the responsibility for Adam's sin? The correct answer to this question is key to the assignment of responsibility for sin by men and fairness by God that free will doctrine demands. I will also discuss more about "God's fairness" in Chapter 12.

As an aside, should anyone try to extrapolate universal salvation from 1 Cor. 15:22, by equating the two "alls" in this verse as being all mankind, the clear context of the whole of Scripture confirms that "all men" will not be saved. Meanwhile, the first "all" of this verse does have to logically include all of mankind, because all of mankind are descendants of Adam and thereby are "by nature the children of wrath."

I emphasize this description of man's nature because no man, by an act of his own will, apart from any working of God's power, can change his nature. Luther stressed the point of the impotence of every man's will due to the deadness of his nature. In the realm of spiritual decisions, a man will not contravene his fallen nature. This is affirmed in 1 Cor. 2: 14:

> 1 Cor. 2:14 But **the natural man receiveth not** the things of the Spirit of God: for they are foolishness unto him: **neither can he know them**, because they are spiritually discerned.

"Can" speaks of ability to do something. In this verse, it defines man's inability to "receive the things of God." Salvation involves the recognition of one's sinfulness, one's helplessness in sin, and one's belief in the truth that death, burial, and resurrection of Jesus Christ, who is the Son of God, is the only way of salvation. All of these recognitions surely qualify as "things of the Spirit of God." As such, they are truths that must be spiritually discerned (received). If lost men are, as Eph. 2:3 has told us, "by nature children of wrath," then 1 Cor. 2:14 has told us what natural man, apart from the work of the Holy Spirit, cannot do—which is to receive "the things of the Spirit of God." Lost men should call to God just like the elderly person in the commercial who cries out, "Help, I've fallen and I can't get up!" But unlike the elderly person, lost men do not realize that they have fallen. By their own wills alone, they do not cry for help.

Then it should be asked, why does God command all men to repent and to believe when He knows they can't? This is a fair question. Although men believe it is well within their ability to understand and choose to believe, I suggest that God, in 1 Cor. 2:14, is revealing to those He has saved the fact that unless He had supernaturally intervened, they would never have believed. In this way, God was revealing the fact that it was by His grace alone that anyone was (or will be) saved. God will later reveal that it was by an act of grace exercised before the beginning of time (Eph. 1:4). 1 Cor. 2:14 is a hint from God about gaining salvation. It is saying, in a somewhat subtle way, "You can't get there from here without spiritual discernment." The next question that should arise from this verse is, "How do I get this discernment when I've just been told I can't do it on my own?" God's answer, elsewhere in Scripture is, "By my grace." Jesus' disciples were moved to ask a similar question: "Who then can be saved?" (Matt. 19:25). This happened after He had told them how difficult it was to get into heaven.

> Matt. 19:25 When his disciples heard it, they were exceedingly amazed, saying, <u>Who then can be saved</u>?

Luther went on from his transformative moment to do battle against Catholicism and, more specifically, against the free will-oriented theology that emerged from his principle opponent, Erasmus. From J.I. Packer's and O.R. Johnson's introduction to their translation of Luther's masterful work, *The Bondage of the Will*, the following excerpts capture the crux of Luther's rebuttal of Arminian theology as championed by Erasmus. Packer and Johnson wrote:

> Historically, it is a simple matter of fact that Martin Luther, and John Calvin, and for that matter, Ulrich Zwingli, Martin Bucer, and all of the leading Protestant theologians of the first epoch of the Reformation, stood on precisely the same ground here. On other points, they had their differences; but in asserting the helplessness of man in sin, and the sovereignty of God in grace, they were entirely at one. To all of them, these doctrines were the very life-blood of the Christian faith. A modern editor of Luther's great work underscores this fact: "Whoever puts this book down without having realized that evangelical theology stands or falls with the doctrine of the bondage of the will has read it in vain." The doctrine of free justification by faith only, which became the storm-centre of so much controversy during the Reformation period, is often regarded as the heart of the reformer's theology, but this is hardly accurate. The truth is that their thinking was really centered upon the contention of Paul, echoed with

varying degrees of adequacy by Augustine and Gottschalk, and Bradwardine and Wycliffe, that the sinner's entire salvation is by free and sovereign grace only. The doctrine of justification by faith was important to them because it safeguarded the principle of sovereign grace; but it actually expressed for them only one aspect of this principle, and that not its deepest aspect. The sovereignty of grace found expression in their thinking at a profounder level still, in the doctrine of monergistic regeneration—the doctrine, that is, that the faith which receives Christ for justification is itself the free gift of a sovereign God, bestowed by spiritual regeneration in the act of effectual calling.[2]

Packer and Johnson continue to assault Arminianism by writing,

Arminianism was, indeed, in Reformed eyes a renunciation of New Testament Christianity in favour of New Testament Judiasm; for to rely on oneself for faith is no different in principle from relying on oneself for works, and the one is as un-Christian and anti-Christian as the other.[3]

Packer and Johnson close their introduction with a challenge to all Christians of their day by writing,

Do we still believe that doctrine matters? Or do we now, as Erasmus, rate a deceptive appearance of unity as of more importance than truth? Have we not grown used to an Erasmian brand of teaching from our pulpits—a message that rests on the same shallow synergistic conceptions which Luther refuted, picturing God and man approaching each other almost on equal terms, each having his own contribution to make to man's salvation and each depending on the dutiful co-operation of the other for the attainment of that end?—as if God exists for man's convenience, rather than man for God's glory?[4]

---

2 J. I. Packer and O. R. Johnson, trans. *The Bondage of the Will*. By Martin Luther. (Old Tappan, NJ: Fleming H. Revell, 1957), 58.
3 Ibid., 59.
4 Ibid, 60.

This is a totally appropriate challenge to Christians today. It is a challenge to which I give a hearty "amen." I believe there is a preponderance of churches and denominations today that have been infected with this "Arminian (free will) flu."

## Jonathan Edwards (1703–1758)

Jonathan Edward's seminal book, *The Freedom of the Will*, delves into the physiological and psychological operation of man's will as it relates to his moral and mental ability to believe the gospel, apart from the moving of an elective influence of God in the heart of man through His Word. He specifically took issue with the degree of, and the meaning of, the adjective "free" as it is applied to a man's will. His zeal for the debate between the sovereignty of God versus the will of man regarding salvation helped spark what is known as "The Great Awakening" of the eighteenth century. Edwards demonstrates the thrust of his treatise writing:

> To talk of the determination of the will, supposes an effect which must have a cause. If the will is to be determined, there is a determiner. This must be supposed to be intended even by them that say the will determines itself. If it be so, the will is both determiner and determined; it is a cause that acts and produces effects upon itself and is the object of its own influence and action.[5]

Edwards continues,

> With respect to that grand inquiry, *What determines the will?*, it would be very tedious and unnecessary at present to enumerate and examine all of the various opinions which have been advanced concerning this matter; nor is it needful that I should enter into a particular disquisition of all points debated in disputes on that question, *Whether they will always follows the last dictate of the understanding*. It is sufficient to

---

5 Jonathon Edwards, *The Freedom of the Will.* (Morgan, PA: Soli Deo Gloria Publications, 1996), 6.

my present purpose to say, *It is that motive which, as it stands in the view of the mind, is the strongest, that determines the will.*[6]

Edward's clarifies his view of man's will in these two excerpts:

The choice of the mind never departs from that which, at the time, and with respect to the direct and immediate objects of that decision of the mind, appears most agreeable and pleasing, all things considered.[7]

There is scarcely a plainer and more universal dictate of the sense and experience of mankind, than that, when men act voluntarily, and do what they please, then they do what suits them best, or what is most *agreeable to them*.[8]

In essence, Edwards points out that man doesn't make choices without a reason. The existence of any choice requires that there are options available. A choice may be a personal preference choice, a physical limitation choice, or a moral choice based upon the conscience that every man possesses to distinguish right and wrong. In short, Edwards says that there are no choices made in a vacuum. All choices have some degree of context and consequences. He writes about the reality of and influence of natural and moral necessities, along with natural and moral inabilities, both of which are directing forces in the choices of man's will. Regarding necessities, Edwards writes:

The phrase *moral necessity* is used variously; sometimes it is used for a necessity of moral obligation. So, we say that a man is under necessity, when he is under bonds of duty and conscience, which he cannot be discharged from.[9]

---

6 Ibid.
7 Ibid., 13.
8 Ibid., 14.
9 Ibid., 24.

> By natural necessity, as applied to men, I mean such necessity as men are under through the force of natural causes; as distinguished from what are called moral causes such as habits and dispositions of the heart and moral motives and inducements. Thus, men placed in certain circumstances are the subjects of particular sensations by necessity; they feel pain when their bodies are wounded.[10]

Regarding inabilities, Edwards continues:

> What has been said of natural and moral necessity, may serve to explain what is intended by natural and moral inability. We are said to be naturally unable to do a thing, when we cannot do it if we will because of what is commonly called nature does not allow it, or because of some impeding defect or obstacle that is extrinsic to the will; either in the faculty of understanding, constitution of the body or external objects. Moral inability consists not of any of these things; but either in the want of inclination or the strength of a contrary inclination, or the want of sufficient motives in view to induce or excite the act of the will, or the strength of apparent motives to the contrary.[11]

It is the action of the will in the moral realm that is the concern of the current debate. The biblical reality of man's moral nature must be correctly perceived in order to rightly understand the moral ability and inability each man has in the exercise of his will. The fact that, as Edwards says, men always choose, naturally and morally, the most preferential of all available options, must be coupled with the biblical truth that fallen men, by nature, view themselves as gods, ruling over their own lives and making their choices according to their own "self-god" wills. In Genesis we are told that man's nature was transformed according to the pronouncement of Satan who told Adam that "ye shall be as gods" (Gen. 3:5). As Edward's points out, it is man's physical

---

10 Ibid.
11 Ibid., 28.

and moral nature that is the determiner of what his will wants. Although Satan lied to Adam and Eve when he said they would not surely die, he was not lying when he told them the outcome of their being "as gods" if they would eat of the forbidden fruit. The extent of man's transformation that occurred when Adam fell was significant and permanent.

> Gen. 3:5 For God doth know that in the day ye eat thereof, then your eyes shall be opened, and <u>ye shall be as gods, knowing good and evil</u>.

In Edwards's day, science and natural theology were being filtered into religious thinking. While the Enlightenment period drove some contemporary theologians toward materialism and a faith in man's power of reason, Edwards saw the growth and discoveries in natural science as confirmations of God's order and wisdom in nature. But, he would not let man's theological reasoning encroach on the truths of God's Word.

Edwards's acceptance of God's prerogative to save some men while passing over others occurred between 1720 and 1726. In 1723 he wrote in his diary, "I made salvation the main business of my life." There was a tendency toward Arminian theology that was existent in the New England colonies. But, by 1729, Edwards, being a strong Calvinist, carried on the battle, preaching and writing against Arminianism. He embarked on a study of the process of conversion in all its phases and varieties, and he recorded his observations with psychological minuteness and discernment, culminating in his most famous book, The Freedom of the Will, in 1754.

### Jerome Zanchius (1516—1590)

The third influential book that I read on the subject of God's sovereignty was written by the Italian reformer Jerome Zanchius and was titled *Absolute Predestination*. Zanchius lived and wrote in the zenith of the Reformation. Born and raised in

Catholicism, as most of the reformers were, he came to grasp the reality of God's grace under the teaching of Peter Martyr, as Martyr expounded upon the Epistle to the Romans. Adding to his studies the teachings of Augustine, Zanchius's theology was transformed, and it moved him out of the Catholic Church and into the newly formed Protestant movement. Typical of many reformers, persecution trailed him around Europe as he moved from pastorate to pastorate. His book on predestination is one of the most solid defenses of the biblical evidences of God's sovereignty, as well as a documenting of the virtual necessity of it. It is worth noting that both Augustine and Martin Luther were also led to God's revelation about salvation by faith alone through the grace of God by studying Paul's letter to the Romans.

Zanchius's book is divided into two sections. The first section is titled "On the Divine Attributes of God," which includes subsections that address God's wisdom and foreknowledge, His will, His unchangeableness, His omnipotence, His justice, and His mercy. The second section of his book is titled "The Doctrine of Absolute Predestination." The subsections to this part of his book cover the definition of the doctrine of predestination, the doctrine as it regards all men, the doctrine as it relates to the saints of God (the elect), the doctrine as it relates to reprobation, and finally why the doctrine (of predestination) should be preached. Zanchius very methodically addresses every subsection by making numerous position statements within each subsection and then supplying his own very cohesive logic to God's predestinating methodology, along with some pertinent Scriptures, to support each of his position statements.

As an example of Zanchius's logical and scriptural support of his various declared positions relating to the subject of predestination, I offer the following two examples.

The first example I offer is where Zanchius postulates about the cause as to why some men are not chosen to salvation. Then he follows his postulation with his reasoned logic that is based upon his understanding of how the God of Scripture acts among men and includes some scriptures that support his conclusions.

> Position 4. As the future faith and good works of the elect were not the cause of their being chosen, so neither were the future sins of the reprobate the cause of their being passed by, but both the choice of the former and the doctrine of omission of the latter were owing, merely and entirely, to the sovereign will and determined pleasure of God.

> We distinguish between preterition (the passing over by God), or bare non-election, which is purely a negative thing, and condemnation, or appointment to punishment: the will of God was the cause of the former, the sins of the non-elect are the cause of the latter. Though God determined to leave, actually does leave, whom He pleases in the spiritual darkness and death of nature, out of which He is under no obligation to deliver them, yet He does not positively condemn any of these merely because He hath not chosen them, but because they have sinned against Him. (see Rom. 1:21–24; Rom. 2:8–9; 2Thess. 2:12) Their preterition or non-inscription in in the Book of Life is not unjust on the part of God, because out of a world of rebels, equally involved in guilt, God (who might, without any impeachment of His justice, have passed by all, as He did with the reprobate angels) was most unquestionably, at liberty, if it so pleased Him, to extend the scepter of His clemency to some and to pitch upon whom He would as the objects of it (His clemency). Nor was this exemption of some any injury to the non-elect, whose case would have been just as bad as it is, even supposing the others had not been chosen at all. Again, the condemnation of the ungodly (for it is under that character alone that they are the subjects of punishment and were ordained to it) is not unjust, seeing it is for sin and only for sin. None are or will be punished but for their iniquities, and all iniquity is properly meritorious of punishment:

where then, is the supposed unmercifulness, tyranny or injustice of the Divine procedure?[12]

Second example: One of the common charges made by free will advocates against any predestinating work of God, whereby some of all mankind are chosen to salvation while the remainder are passed over (not chosen), is their accusation that, if predestination was true, it would make God the author of sin. This charge says that God created them to be reprobate from eternity, ergo, He is the creator of the sin of sinful man. Here is how Zanchius rebuts this charge against God:

> Position 5. God is the creator of the wicked, but not their wickedness; He is the author of their being, but not the infuser of their sin.
>
> It is most certainly His will (for adorable and unsearchable reasons) to permit sin, but with all possible reverence be it spoken, it should seem that He cannot, consistently with the purity of His nature, the glory of His attributes, and the truth of His declarations, be Himself the author of it (sin). "Sin" says the apostle "entered into the world by one man," meaning Adam, consequently it was not introduced by the Deity Himself. Though without the permission of His will and the concurrence of His providence, its introduction had been impossible, yet is He not hereby the Author of sin so introduced.* (*a Zanchius footnote: "It is known and a very just maxim of the schools, 'An effect follows from, and is to be ascribed to, the last immediate cause that produced it.' Thus, for instance, if I hold a book or a stone in my hand, my holding it is the immediate cause of its not falling; but if I let it go, my letting it go is not the immediate cause of its falling: it is carried downwards by its own gravity which is therefore the causa proxima effectus, the proper and immediate cause of its descent. It is true, if I had kept my hold of it, it would not

---

12 Jerome Zanchius, *Absolute Predestination* (Grand Rapids: Sovereign Grace Publishers, Inc., 1971), 74–75.

have fallen, yet still the immediate, direct cause of its fall is its own weight, not my quitting my hold. The application of this to the providence of God, as concerned in sinful events, is easy. Without God, there could have been no creation; without creation, no creatures, without creatures, no sin. Yet sin is not chargeable on God: for effectus sequitur causam proximam. (effect follows the nearest cause) Luther observes (De Servo Arbito cap.42) "It is a great degree of faith to believe that God is merciful and gracious, though He saves so few and condemns so many, and that He is strictly just, though, in consequence of His own will, He made us not exempt from liableness to condemnation." (De Servo Arbito cap.48): "Although God doth not make sin, nevertheless He ceases not to create and multiply individuals in the human nature, which, through the withholding of His Spirit, is corrupted by sin, just as a skillful artist may form curious statues out of bad materials. So, such as their nature is, such are men themselves; God forms them out of such a nature."[13]

These are two typical examples of the format that Zanchius uses throughout his solid case for the absolute sovereignty of God in the act of salvation. I highly recommend his book to any reader who wants to pursue a deeper investigation into the question of how a man is saved.

### Thomas Watson, (c. 1620–1689 or 1690)

Thomas Watson, an eminent Puritan minister of the 1600s, delivered 176 sermons focused on the catechism of the Westminster Assembly. In 1692, a few years after his death, these sermons were compiled and published by C.H. Spurgeon under the title, *A Body of Divinity*. Within his expositions on forty-two topics of the catechism, which contain a multitude of biblically extracted doctrines, is a thought provoking section on the fall. I share some of his insights on the fall and Adam's sin that are pertinent to the topic of this book—man's will.

---

13 Ibid., 75–76.

## A BRIEF HISTORICAL PERSPECTIVE

At the beginning of the section on the fall, Watson points out that God created Adam (all mankind) under "covenant of works" with His command in Gen. 2:16–17. It regards the permission to eat freely of any tree in the garden except the Tree of the Knowledge of Good and Evil. The conditions were simple: eat not of the forbidden tree and live, or eat of it and "thou shalt surely die."

Watson makes a profound point about this covenant of works. Updated in modern language, he taught,

> The covenant of works was not built on a very firm basis; and therefore must needs leave men full of tears and doubt. The covenant of works rested upon the strength of man's inherent righteousness, which though in innocence was perfect, yet was subject to change. Adam was created holy, but mutable; having the power to stand and a power to fall.[14]

This mutability confirms a significant difference between God's image and man's image. This will be discussed later in the book

Watson states,

> Whosoever they are that look for righteousness and salvation by the power of their free will, or inherent goodness of their nature, or by virtue of their merit, as the Socinians and the Papists, they are all under the covenant of works.[15]

The point I want to draw from Watson's teaching about man being created under a covenant of works is that this covenant of works continues to this day. Unbelievers naturally remain committed to following hard after the dictates of their fallen nature. But it is worth noting that the whole of the biblical relationship between God and man is told in the context of this works covenant, up to the place where the covenant (dispensation) of grace

---

14 Thomas Watson, *A Body of Divinity*. (London: Banner of Truth Trust, 1965), 130.

15 Ibid., 131.

is revealed through the apostle Paul. Adam, Abraham, Moses, the kings, and the prophets of Israel all had their commands for obedience to God. The twelve disciples and the Pentecostal Jewish church of Acts 2 had their marching orders in a works context.

What is the point of this long-running covenant of works? I propose that it is a parallel point to the law. Paul gives the purpose of both in Romans:

> Rom. 3:20 Therefore by the deeds of the law [works] there shall no flesh be justified in his sight: <u>for by the law is the knowledge of sin.</u>

The distilled truth of this verse is that no works can justify man in God's sight and that His law clarifies the truth of what offends God—sin. Up to the time of God's rescue by the covenant of grace, the futility of reaching God's requirement of perfection under the covenant of self-generated works, including free will belief, makes heaven unattainable. The mystery that salvation by grace is received only by God's grace of revelation to His elect is still unrecognized by the free will adherents. Free will (Arminian) Christians cling to the power of their will as the key that unlocked their salvation. This clinging, in turn, causes most such Christians to consciously or subconsciously mix some degree of, and form of, works into their salvation theology. Dependence upon any sort of personal work will engender some degree of self-doubt, i.e., "Did I do enough?" Even free will belief leaves a person susceptible to the thought of, "Did I really believe?" or "Was I sincere enough?" They can never answer these doubts because they are trying to measure an unknowable quantity.

Watson goes on to make some essential biblical observations about Adam. Quoting Solomon in Eccl. 7:29:

> Eccl. 7:29 Lo, this only have I found, that God hath made man upright; but they have sought out many inventions.

## A BRIEF HISTORICAL PERSPECTIVE

Watson says, "Adam was perfectly holy, he had rectitude of mind and liberty of will to do good, but his head ached till he had invented his own and our death, he sought out many inventions."[16] I can't confirm the headache from Scripture, but Adam was restless and easily tempted from his perfect righteous state as he was created. Watson notes that Adam's fall was voluntary and it was sudden. Watson reinforces his suggestion that it was sudden by the fact that Adam and Eve had not yet eaten of the Tree of Life, else they would have possessed eternal life. Perhaps they were on their way to it but got distracted by the serpent at the Tree of Knowledge.

It is stated in the Psalms that man abandoned his position:

> Ps. 49:12 <u>Nevertheless man being in honour abideth not</u>: he is like the beasts that perish.

The beasts have no choice but to perish. Not so with Adam and all mankind in him. He, and we, had a choice. Adam, a holy creation of God with an unbiased power of his own will to "do right and live" or to "do evil and die," could not stand in the right when left on his own. Adam's failure testifies to the truth that Jesus spoke in John 15:5: *For without me ye can do nothing.*

How proud, then, can Christians be today to presume that they can do on their own what Adam could not—obey by belief of their own will to salvation. From Genesis to today, men hear God asking them to "do" things that they are physically able to do but are spiritually unwilling to do, perfectly. This dilemma cries for a savior.

This commentary on the covenant of works and the fall of Adam are mere samples of Mr. Watson's ability to divide and extrapolate Christian doctrine. Whether or not one agrees with the entirety of Thomas Watson's multifaceted dissertations of the doctrines of the Westminster Assembly, this collection of

---

16 Ibid., 137.

Watson's sermons is a worthwhile read for anyone who wants to wade into deeper doctrinal waters than most pastors will ever lead them.

The four aforementioned theologians provide solid testimony for the place of God's sovereignty in the salvation of any man.

### An Arminian Opponent: Dr. Laurence M. Vance

It is definitely beneficial for any interested reader to review the history of this debate to get a feel for the depth of it. I will not provide the history in any deeper detail here. Many more learned scholars than me have already done the legwork on that task. Dr. Laurence M. Vance is one such scholar. Having provided a sampling of the writings of five notable proponents of God's sovereignty in salvation, I will now turn to the free will side of the issue and give the reader a review of the fifth book I read. It was written by Dr. Vance and titled *The Other Side of Calvinism*. As the title hints, Dr. Vance comes to the debate in clear opposition to the sovereignty view (commonly called Calvinism). I recommend his book to any reader who wants a very thorough recounting of the historic evolution of the battle between Calvinism and Arminianism. In his preface, Dr. Vance clearly states the purpose of this 652-page (including appendices) book. He writes,

> There still exists the need for a definitive work which addresses and sufficiently answers all of the philosophical speculations and theological implications of the other side of Calvinism. A shortage of works against Calvinism is not an adequate reason to begin an undertaking of this magnitude unless there be an important underlying cause. The salient determinant is the tremendously damaging nature of the Calvinistic system. The doctrines of Calvinism, *if really believed and consistently*

*practiced*, are detrimental to evangelism, personal soul winning, prayer, preaching and practical Christianity in general.[17]

Dr. Vance is not subtle in his charges against Calvinism, which he says is also labeled "the doctrines of grace" in some religious circles. He goes on to specifically define his reasons for writing his lengthy rebuttal of Calvinism by writing,

> Calvinism is therefore the greatest "Christian" heresy that has ever plagued the Church. This being the case, the thesis of this book is that Calvinism is not only Reformed doctrine and therefore is something that Baptists should not be connected with, but *that* it is *wrong* doctrine.[18]

> Let me unequivocally assert that the purpose of this book is to show that Calvinism is beyond all doubt *not* the teaching of the Bible nor of reason[19]

I would add here in rebuttal to Dr. Vance's "greatest heresy" charge against Calvinism, that Calvinists would be equally entitled to level the same charge against Arminianism. With regard to heresy, it becomes an accusatory standoff. The only true arbiter of truth and heresy is Scripture. The challenge to believers is the successful discrediting of one or the other of the accusations. In this debate, they can't both be heresies.

Despite Dr. Vance's emphatic anti-sovereignty (anti-Calvinist) position, I recommend his book to my readers for two reasons. In the first 183 pages of his book, Dr. Vance provides a most thorough documentation of the evolution of the controversy between Calvinism (sovereignty) versus Arminianism (free will). Even though his Calvinist animosity is revealed in many

---

17 Laurence M. Vance, *The Other Side of Calvinism*, (Vance Publications): 2002 revised edition p. ix-x.

18 Vance, x.
19 Ibid.

places, Dr. Vance provides readers with a detailed background of the path that this debate has followed, up to the revised second printing of his book in 2002. The history and intricate depth of this major doctrinal dispute among Christians is fascinating but also dismaying, due to the stark doctrinal division that still remains between so many Christians.

The second reason for recommending this book is simply to understand the typical, but specific, free will rebuttals that Dr. Vance puts forward in his passionate attack against the sovereignty view. If one is going to ever seek the correct answer to this debate, they have to clearly hear all the points of the opponent's arguments. Otherwise, too much time can be spent arguing about what the other side did or did not say. I will not counter every argument that Dr. Vance postulates against the sovereignty position, but instead, I will try to distill my rebuttal to what I feel is the essence of his arguments against Calvinism. I will also offer some pertinent Scriptures and my exposition of them, which I believe will refute Dr. Vance's Arminian (free will) case.

Dr. Vance provides a very representative view of the Arminian (free will) position. In the second and major section of his book, pages 185 to 596, Dr. Vance documents the specific history of the evolution of the five points of Calvinism, which represent the summarized description of Calvinist doctrine that Dr. Vance calls "the greatest Christian heresy." He goes into a lengthy, point by point dissection of each of the five points of Calvinism. He documents the varied and sometimes contradictory positions that Calvinists through the ages have produced regarding each point. He is also careful to insert his free will (Arminian) defense against every Calvinist point. Dr. Vance's book is exhaustively footnoted at the end of the book, stretching from page 653 to page 740. His bibliography is 20 pages long, while his indexes are divided by subject, name and verse, covering pages 761 to 788.

Dr. Vance's book is a very comprehensive critique against Calvinism and God's total sovereignty in salvation. There are many other anti-Calvinist books available, despite Dr. Vance's contention of there being a shortage of such books. But I doubt that there is a more comprehensive treatise than his which opposes the Calvinist or sovereignty side of this great divide. (I will offer comments from two other Arminian leaning books and authors in Chapter 8.)

CHAPTER 4

# A Critique of Dr. Vance's The Other Side of Calvinism

**The Origin of the Five Points of Calvinism**

TO ATTACK CALVINISM, ONE must attack the TULIP acronym that is synonymous with Calvinism. Dr. Vance provides a thorough documentation of this foundational doctrinal layout of the Calvinist system of theology. He gives a detailed account of where the bulb for this theological "flower" came from and of the ground where it was planted.

The five points of Calvinism have been a major source of contention in this doctrinal battle ever since they were issued at the Synod of Dort in 1619. I have biblically tested and wrestled with these points ever since they came to my knowledge years ago in my Christian walk. For any reader who is not familiar with them, they represent what Dr. Vance calls, "the sum and substance of the Calvinistic system."[20] They are historically referred to by the acronym TULIP.

T = total depravity
U = unconditional election
L = limited atonement
I = irresistible grace
P = perseverance of the saints

It is the theology of these five points that the counter-remonstrants published in response to the Dutch remonstrants who did not agree with the doctrine of the predestination of men to salvation. Instead, the Dutch remonstrants have taken the topic of predestination, as revealed in Ephesians and elsewhere, to mean the predestinating of believers to other things, but not the predestining of believers themselves. This is a subtle distinction, but it is one that carries great interpretative significance. It is ironic that the label that has been perpetually affixed to the remonstrants' view of predestination is "Arminianism." Jacobus Arminius died in 1609, ten years before the Synod of Dort produced the theological positions represented by the TULIP. Dr. Vance tells us that Arminius was "just as orthodox on the cardinal doctrines of the Christian Faith as any Calvinist, ancient or modern."[21]

Arminius never wrote any theological commentaries similar to Calvin's magnum opus titled, *Institutes of the Christian Religion*. However, when the doctrine of predestination began to be promoted within the Dutch Reformed Church, and ministers began to publish books in opposing views about predestination, Arminius, being a prominent theologian of his day, received two requests. He was asked to refute the anti-Calvinist writings by some Dutch ministers, but he was also asked to (and ultimately persuaded to) write a refutation of some writings that supported the Calvinistic view. Dr. Vance relates the irony of this event in

---

20 Vance, 143.
21 Vance, 126.

the life of Arminius. Dr. Vance tells us that it was during this writing effort that Arminius underwent a theological transformation and "became a convert to the very opinions he (at one time) had been requested to refute."[22] Although the account of his entry into the predestination fray is muddled, Dr. Vance wrote,

> The fact is that Arminuis was now publicly on record as being opposed to the established Calvinism of the Reformed Church.[23]

The controversy over predestination did not die with the death of Arminius in 1609. It grew. The "Arminian" contingent, if you will, pushed for the acceptance of their views in the Dutch Reformed Church to the point where a national synod was called to resolve the debate. Because of the existence of the church-state form of government in that day, any synod (ecclesiastical council) involved political, as well as theological, elements. In 1610, forty-six pro-Arminian ministers drew up the remonstrance (protest) against Calvinism and presented it to the Synod of Dort, in which they were participants. The Calvinist counter-remonstrators produced the answer to the Arminian remonstrance that, among other things, set forth the basic five points that would become what is historically called the Calvinist TULIP. Since the Calvinists had the political upper hand in that day, Dr. Vance relates,

> It comes as no surprise that the synod condemned the Arminian tenets as unscriptural and issued the infamous canons of Dort in 1619, setting forth the Five Points of Calvinism[24]

As we know from Church history, the fires of this debate have not yet been quenched. The war between the Calvinist

---

22 Vance, 134.
23 Ibid.
24 Vance, 154.

(sovereignty of God) theology and the Arminian (free will of man) theology is alive and well today. Theologians are in general agreement that it was the subject of predestination that ignited this war, and it was St. Augustine (354 to 430 AD) who fired the first significant shot in this war. Dr. Vance cites four prominent theologians who declare the fact of Augustine's influence on John Calvin's theology.[25] Augustine, in his famous writing *Confessions*, offered a startling declaration that ignited a battle with a fellow theologian, Pelagius (390 to 418 AD). When Augustine wrote of God, "Give what thou commandest and command what thou will," it infuriated Pelagius, who felt such a statement made man a mere puppet of God. According to Dr. Vance, Pelagius taught that:

> When Adam fell it had no effect on his posterity; the only relation of Adam's sin to the human race is that of a bad example.[26]

Thus, the predestination battle was on. Pelagius, although he never personally met Augustine, would become Augustine's principle opponent, much like Erasmus was to Luther, and Arminius was to Calvin.

Dr. Vance, in his substantial dissertation against God's sovereignty in salvation, gives quotations from three of the four Calvinist authors I have quoted: Luther, Edwards, and Zanchius. Luther is quoted thirty-one times, Edwards is quoted seven times and Zanchius is quoted three times in Dr. Vance's book. (It is startling that Thomas Watson's writings are not found in Dr. Vance's nineteen-page bibliography.) Dr. Vance's quotes from these men are accurate and are used to document the Calvinist position. The views of these three men, as well as many other reformers, are used by Dr. Vance to portray what he sees as the

---

25 Vance, 37–38.
26 Vance, 51.

variations among Calvinistic views, which thereby sets up his own rebuttal against the essential five points of Calvinism.

**Dissecting the TULIP**

To further examine Dr. Vance's comprehensive cross-examination of the five points of Calvinism and the Arminian objections to it, I will survey his in-depth, petal by petal critique of the TULIP.

As I read Dr. Vance's lengthy dissection of each of the five points that summarize the foundational doctrines of Calvinism, it struck me that his main arguments with the first four doctrinal points were primarily directed at the adjectives that modify them. The terms depravity, election, atonement, and grace are doctrinal, biblical topics with which Dr. Vance has no quarrel. The Calvinistic adjectives of total, unconditional, and irresistible fueled the Reformation and the resulting battle that continues to this day. On the Arminian side, it is only one adjective, free, which is perpetually used to modify the word "will," that is the principal point of contention for the sovereignty advocates. I will examine the use of this adjective in depth in Chapters 5 through 8.

After his most thorough recounting of the history of the split between those who defend God's sovereignty in salvation and those who insist that man is still able to exercise an operative free will to accept or reject the gospel, Dr. Vance proceeds to a point by point dissection of the five points of Calvinism. Early in his examination of the first point, Total Depravity, Dr. Vance makes a contextual observation about it in relation to the other five points. He writes,

> Total Depravity is one of the three essential points of Calvinism, the other two being Unconditional Election and Irresistible Grace. These three points are the essence of the Calvinistic system. The denial of the other two points, Limited

Atonement and the Perseverance of the Saints, does not affect the basic premise of Calvinism.[27]

I agree with this conclusion by Dr. Vance. The two points he mentions in this excerpt that do not affect the basic premise of Calvinism, are two points to which I also object. Like Dr. Vance, I reject the *"P"* position of Calvinism, which asserts the teaching that all of the elect who have been regenerated by God will persevere in the faith. This was the first petal of the TULIP that I rejected as it was stated. Whatever the Calvinists meant by the term "perseverance," the point to be made is that it speaks to a work of man. Perseverance is a subjective metric that evaluates one's life against some perceived biblical standard of behavior. Think about the apostle Peter at the moment of his third denial of Jesus when the rooster crowed. What if Peter had died at this moment? Would his lack of perseverance have called his salvation into question?

As such, perseverance gives no credit to God. As I thought about it, we know that some believers falter in their faith and thus, in the eyes of others, do not persevere and even die in such a state. So, if the letter *P* in the TULIP must be retained, I would transplant the *P* of Perseverance with the *P* of Preservation, which is another sovereign activity of God. Jesus affirmed this activity of the Father when He said,

> John 6:39 And this is the Father's will which hath sent me, that <u>of all which he hath given me I should lose nothing, but should raise it up again at the last day</u>.
>
> John 10:28 And I give unto them eternal life; and <u>they shall never perish, neither shall any man pluck them out of my hand</u>.

---

27 Vance, p. 190

> 2 Tim. 4:18 And the <u>Lord shall deliver me</u> from every evil work, <u>and will preserve me unto his heavenly kingdom</u>: to whom be glory for ever and ever. Amen.

Preservation is a work of the Father that is assured. Thankfully, a believer's perseverance has nothing to do with their preservation. God wants us to persevere, but He knows that the fallen nature of humans still causes them to stumble in their faith. Paul lamented his own inconsistency of perseverance in Romans 7. God provides believers the power to persevere, but He does not make them persevere. Sadly, it is true that some believers falter badly in their Christian walk, even to the extent of dying with little evidence of their salvation having been observed by others. John 6:39 and John 10:28, apart from declaring that those who are Christ's were given to Him by the Father, plainly tells us that none of those who were given to Jesus can ever be lost. This negates any possibility of being lost by any failure of perseverance on their part. God preserves their salvation, but not their persevering walk in this life. The lack of a believer's perseverance in his Christian walk in this life will be dealt with at the rewards judgment at the Bema Seat of Christ. This is another part of the mystery revealed only through Paul.

The other TULIP letter that Dr. Vance dismissed as non-essential is the *L* of Limited Atonement. This assertion is one that has caused great (and needless) controversy among Calvinists and Arminians through the ages. I say it is needless because both sides can scripturally defend it, but not in the same context. Arminians are correct to scripturally reject it as Calvinism presents it because the Bible clearly states that Christ's death was an atonement for all men.

Rom. 5:6 For when we were yet without strength, in due time <u>Christ died for the ungodly</u>. (Who are the ungodly? All mankind.)

Rom. 5:18 Therefore as by the offence of one judgment came upon all men to condemnation; even so <u>by the righteousness of one **the free gift came upon all men** unto justification of life</u>.

However, Calvinists can justify "limited atonement" in either an "after-the-fact" context or in a "before-the-fact" context of the atonement. After-the-fact, in its ultimate effect, Christ's atoning work will only accrue to the benefit of God's elect. Before the fact, an omniscient God knew that Christ's atonement would be limited in its effect because His sovereign choices for salvation were made before the beginning of the world. God knows this, but men can never know it in this life. But, these two facts did not prevent the offer of atonement from being made to all men. Because men do not know who will be saved, they cannot know who will receive the benefit. From either perspective, Limited Atonement is an inflammatory and unnecessary assertion. The assertion of Limited Atonement as a doctrine degrades the truth that Christ died for all men. It only serves to give Arminians their strongest point of argument in the TULIP debate. Even though it ruins the convenient acronym TULIP, I discard the L because it is indefensible and it distorts the point of the argument. (The acronym evaporates, but the doctrinal truth remains.)

The crux of Dr. Vance's criticism of Calvinist doctrine and the launching point for his book is found at the end of his introduction. After offering his preliminary objections to Calvinism, vis-à-vis Arminianism, Vance concludes his "Introduction to Calvinism" chapter by writing,

"So what it all comes down to is this: Are men elected to salvation or are they not? That is the issue among Christians. The issue is not, as Warfield says, that "there are fundamentally only two doctrines of salvation: that salvation is from God, and that salvation is from ourselves". No Christian disagrees with that, although that is how a Calvinist will shift the issue to make his system look like it alone teaches salvation by grace. Wilson is even more subtle: "What is the decisive factor as to whether or not one is a sovereign gracer or an Arminian as to salvation? It is this: The sovereign gracer teaches that the final decisive factor as to whether or not one is saved is the will and work of God, while the Arminian teaches that the final decisive factor as to whether or not one is saved is the will and/or work of man." Now, no true Christian believes that works have any part in his salvation; however, the role of the will of man is a separate issue. By combining the two, the Calvinist once again implies that only his system teaches salvation by grace. The issue is: election to salvation. All Calvinists, whether they be Presbyterian or Reformed, Primitive Baptist or Sovereign Grace Baptist; all Calvinists whether they be premillennial or amillenial, dispensational or covenant theologist; all Calvinists, whether go by the name or not; all Calvinists have one thing in common: God, by a sovereign, eternal decree, has determined before the foundation of the world who shall be saved and who shall be lost. To obscure the real issue, a vocabulary has been invented to confuse and confound the Christian. The arguments about supralapsarianism and infralapsarianism, total depravity and total inability, reprobation and preterition, synergism and monergism, free will and free agency, common grace and special grace, general calling and effectual calling, perseverance and preservation, and the sovereignty of God are all immaterial. The stumbling block for the Calvinist is the simplicity of salvation, so upon rejecting this, a system has to be constructed whereby salvation is made a mysterious, arcane, incomprehensible, decree of God. Thus, the basic error of Calvinism is confounding election and with salvation, which they never are in the Bible, but only in philosophical speculations and theological implications of Calvinism: the other side of Calvinism.[28]

From this conclusion, Dr. Vance found the title for his book. From here, he sets off to debunk every possible attempt by Calvinism to correlate election with salvation. In his opinion, the truth about election is the issue that will settle this debate. On this point, I won't disagree. If he can biblically disprove this assertion about election, he will win the argument. I, however, argue the exact opposite. I believe the Bible teaches that election and salvation are inseparable as Bible truths.

**Total Depravity**
Here is how Dr. Vance builds his case to refute the Calvinists' "basic error" of salvation that is based solely upon God's sovereign election. He isolates the Calvinist doctrine of Total Depravity as a fatal link in the TULIP string of doctrinal assertions. Vance lays out his point of attack when he writes,

> Total Depravity necessitates the doctrines of Unconditional Election and Irresistible Grace.[29]

If he were a lawyer in the courtroom, this would be his opening statement: "I will expose the fallacy of the doctrine of Total Depravity and thereby nullify the points of Unconditional Election and Irresistible Grace, which then effectively dismantles the TULIP." I agree with Dr. Vance's contention of Unconditional Election and Irresistible Grace as being dependent upon the validity of the premise of Total Depravity. Why? If it is logically deduced that a man is totally depraved, so as to be truly unable to save himself or even choose to be saved, then God's work of election must be unconditional, or else, as it says in Romans 11:6, otherwise grace is no more grace. Likewise, if it is a

---
28 Vance, 34–35.
29 Vance, 190.

## A CRITIQUE OF DR. VANCE'S THE OTHER SIDE OF CALVINISM

biblical truth that grace is necessary for salvation, then saving grace must be irresistible if man is totally depraved. Thus, disproving Total Depravity as Calvinism proposes it, becomes Dr. Vance's crucial objective. Disproving Total Depravity opens the door for conditional election—that is, election based upon the condition of man's free will act of belief. Disproving Total Depravity also makes God's saving grace resistible by any free will rejection of the offer of salvation. Dr. Vance's mission is clear.

Dr. Vance devotes fifty-five pages to his critique of Total Depravity. Although he might feel that he debunks the point of Total Depravity to his own satisfaction, in the interest of thorough scholarship, he devotes equally ample space to the other four points in his quest to slay the Calvinist dragon. But early on, in page 190, Dr. Vance reasserts his reasoning for his lengthy attack on depravity. He writes,

> If Total Depravity is proven to be spurious, the rest of the TULIP withers.[30]

After Dr. Vance made this profound assertion, I find it curious as to why he devoted as much effort as he does to the remaining four petals of the TULIP in his substantial book. The proposition above is logical in a theological context. If the fact of man's Total Depravity, as Calvinism proposes, is proved untrue, debunking the other points, it seems to me, is unnecessary. All Dr. Vance needs to do is pluck the Total Depravity petal from Calvinism's flower and it dies.

First, consider the point of Unconditional Election. Using an "if. . .then" rationale, the dependence of the doctrines of Unconditional Election and Irresistible Grace upon Total Depravity is easily demonstrated. If man is not so depraved as to be incapable of deciding to believe in his heart, then whatever God's

---

30 Ibid.

work of election means, it must be, in some manner, dependent upon man's free will decision. If the effect of a free will decision upon the act of election by God is true for one, then it must be true for all men. If the free will decision is an inseparable factor of God's election, then it degrades whatever value there is to being one of God's elect. Why? Because the fact of the matter is that if by man's free will he chooses to believe, then truth of election would mean that man actually elects (chooses) himself to become the elect of God—a nonsensical conclusion. It would mean that if God calls anyone his elect, it is because they elected to be the elect. The Bible uses the word "elect" as a noun twenty times in a context which suggests that it is an honored designation given by God to men and angels. If it is just a designation given to men because they elect to be God's elect, there is no real honor to be credited to the term. As stated earlier, this view makes election an obligation of God.

Turning to Irresistible Grace, God's bestowal of His grace upon man has many forms, such as exceptional intelligence, special abilities like a beautiful singing voice or athletic prowess, exceptional beauty, etc. Saving grace, however, is the ultimate grace that God can bestow. But whatever saving grace is, in the Arminian mind, if free will is an operable part of salvation, then saving grace must be resistible. Why? No logical Bible student believes that all men will be saved. As mentioned earlier, the description of hell and the promise of eternal damnation, as frequently mentioned in the Bible, would be an idle threat from God, if hell were not a reality. Thus, the truth of these realities can only mean that those who die unsaved have resisted God's saving grace offer of salvation by the exercise of their free will.

As I previously have shown, the *L* (Limited Atonement) is a futile argument and the *P* of assured Perseverance is an erroneous assertion of Calvinism because it is an accomplishment of the individual. Neither of these petals of the TULIP carries any weight in the argument against the issue of free will. I understand that the *L* and the *P* were constructed in direct rebuttal of the five points of the Dutch remonstrants, but they lose their relevance in the overall Calvinism/Arminian dispute when it is focused on the theological mechanics of salvation.

Total Depravity, is thus the essential point of attack for Dr. Vance and his Arminian brethren for the purpose of disconnecting God's sovereign act of electing men to salvation. The adjective that needs to be closely examined for the purpose of proof (or disproof) of the extent of man's depravity is the word *total*. The bulk of Dr. Vance's attack on this first point of the TULIP is focused on how Calvinists define the word total. He establishes that there can be no objection to the biblical fact of man's depravity. He devotes several pages and quotes several verses to confirm it. He details the historical use of and development of the meaning of this adjective as it is employed by various Calvinists thorough the centuries since the Reformation. Dr. Vance uses the variations of its definition among various Calvinist theologians as proof of their error.

As he nears his concluding paragraphs about Total Depravity, he sets out to prove that man is not unable to believe, as most Calvinist doctrinal positions assert. Vance believes he has the key to overthrow Total Depravity and the verses to prove it. He writes,

> Therefore the principle that overthrows Total Depravity is this: a man may be condemned for his ignorance or his unwillingness, but never for his inability to do what God has commanded him to do."[31]

As it stands, this statement by Dr. Vance is true. What he and Arminianism fail to understand is that man has not always been unable to obey all of God's commands. Adam (all men) was never ignorant, nor unable. But Adam (all men) chose to be unwilling.

---

31 Vance, 236.

**Is Man's Depravity Total?**

Working from the basic Calvinist contention of Total Depravity that fallen man is not able, in and of himself, and apart from the grace of God, to believe God's gospel, Dr. Vance finishes his assault on the adjective *total*, by offering two types of verses that he feels disproves any such inability. The first type are verses in which there is a command to believe. He uses 1 John 3:23 as one such example.

> 1 John 3:23 <u>And this is his commandment,</u> <u>That we should believe</u> on the name of his Son Jesus Christ, and love one another, as he gave us commandment.

It was previously shown using Scripture that when God commanded obedience to something like the Law, only perfect, heart-originated obedience would be acceptable. Dr. Vance believes that God would never command man to do something that is impossible for him to do. I think Dr. Vance could have chosen even better "command" verses than he did. In this age of grace, the Bible commands one thing for man to do to be saved—believe the gospel! In the letters of Paul, who is the apostle for the dispensation of grace (Eph. 3:2), there are twenty-six uses of the word *believe* that are either direct or indirect references to belief in Christ. Recall the simple answer Paul and Silas gave the Philippian jailer to his question about salvation,

> Acts 16:30 And brought them out, and said, Sirs, <u>what must I do to be saved?</u>

> Acts 16:31 And they said, <u>Believe on the Lord Jesus Christ, and thou shalt be saved, and thy house</u>.

It is without question that men are commanded to believe the gospel. Verse 31 provides specific instruction regarding what men are commanded to do to be saved. In verse 30, notice the word "do" in boldface. Notice also the cause and effect connection of these verses. If one wants the effect of verse 30, "be[ing] saved," it must be accomplished by the cause of the action taken in verse 31, "[belief] on the Lord Jesus Christ." The point made here is that the command of belief to men is the standing order of this dispensation for men to obey. The word *do* was highlighted because it is the running theme of the gospel of the age of grace. The thrust of Paul's ministry was that salvation is now through God's grace alone and not through any works of man. Yet, Acts 16:30–31 have clearly told men what they must "do"! Works are something that men "do" to accomplish a goal. Yet, I hear many Christians vigorously insist that belief is not a work of man. I think that Acts 16:30–31 contradicts that premise. The question was "what must I do?" and the answer was "believe."

Jesus also affirmed that belief in Him is a work. Quoting from the gospel of John:

> John 6:28 Then said they unto him, <u>What shall we do, that we might work the works of God?</u>

> John 6:29 Jesus answered and said unto them, **This is the work of God, that ye believe on him whom he hath sent.**

This question by the crowd is a very interesting one. Jesus had, in so many words, been pointing out that the use of their physical needs as a motivation for seeking Him, was wrong. The question about doing "the works of God", is an indication that the crowd had begun to hear Jesus' point. Once Jesus shifted their focus from their physical desires to a spiritual context for their seeking, their Jewish Law mindset kicked in. They wanted to know how they could do "the works of God."

Jesus' answer warrants careful consideration. He said, "This is the work of God, that ye believe on Him [Jesus himself] whom He [God] has sent." Jesus did not say, "This is what you must do to please God." Think about the phrase, "This is the work of God." This "work" means "[belief] on Him whom He has sent." Think about the term "work of God." Creation, healing the sick, raising the dead, dividing the sea, holding back the waters, making the sun stand still; these are some works that only God can do. Man cannot do the works of God. In their fallen state, as their own gods, men think that they can do the work of believing on "Him whom he hath sent" for salvation. They were yet to learn that any faith of their own was insufficient. The truth of verse 29, which makes believing "on him whom he hath sent," a work of God, escapes a large portion of Christianity today. However, it seems logical that people take credit for their believing.

In reiteration, with this answer Jesus made two crucial points. The first was that "believing" was indeed a work. The second (subtle) point was that saving belief was itself, "the work of God." I can't prove it, but I believe that the crowd only understood the first point. The second point went un-comprehended. Jesus plainly called belief a work and challenged the followers to do it. Although the crowd might have thought that they could obey and perform this "work," they would not learn until later, as revealed by Jesus through Paul, that the "work" they thought they could do was really a "work of God" given as a gift (Eph. 2:8–9).

This refutes the persistent argument by many New Testament believers today who say that the act of belief is not a work. Arminians make two errors about the issue of belief. First, they insist that the act of belief is not a work. It is a work that a man must do, but it cannot be done apart from the "work of God" in their hearts. This brings us to the second point. Free Will doctrine fails to concede that saving belief (faith) is gifted by God to "whom He chooses." They may well rebut this point by pointing out the volume of calls from all of the New Testament writers, including Paul, to "believe the gospel." Logic would dictate that if we are commanded to believe, then we must be able to do so.

Here, again, God is teaching the same lesson as He did with Israel when He gave them the Law to obey. In both of these cases God (Jesus) knew that man would not keep the Law nor believe the gospel by the power of his own will. How did Jesus know? He knows what is in all men.

> John 2:25 And needed not that any should testify of man: <u>for he knew what was in man.</u>

In John 8:43, Jesus went so far as to tell the very religious leaders of Israel that they could not understand His teaching because they "cannot hear" His word.

> John 8:43 Why do ye not understand my speech? even because <u>ye cannot hear my word</u>.

Nevertheless, Jesus still proclaimed His word to them.

Jesus reveals this later in chapter 6 of John. He states the reason why man alone cannot "believe" in Him by his will alone:

> John 6:65 And he said, Therefore said I unto you, that <u>no man can come unto me, except it were given unto him of my Father</u>.

This response from Jesus drove many of the followers away either in confusion or discouragement. However, if the truths of John 6:29, 6:65 and 8:43 are considered together, they confirm the later truth that Paul reveals in Eph. 2:8–9, that faith (belief) is (and must be) a gift of God. While belief is still a work or act of a man, it cannot be produced solely by the power of their own will. This work can only occur by the efficacious working of God, the Spirit, in man. That working is a sovereign work of God. (In literature, this would be an example of a "deus ex machna" device in the biblical narrative." (See Appendix ** for the definition.)

Belief is clearly an action that man "does" throughout all of their life. Children believe their parents. Parents, occasionally, believe their children. We sometimes look at the sky and say, "I believe it I going to rain." We drive over a bridge that we have never crossed, believing that it will hold the weight of our vehicle. We believe a good friend who says, "trust me." We believe our sweetheart when he or she says, "I love you." We do these acts of belief and many more, entirely of our own accord. Nobody can do it for us. We always have the choice—believe it or not, as Ripley puts it.

Often, belief choices are influenced by certain evidences—believing it is going to rain because of the dark clouds on the horizon or driving over a bridge because you see other traffic using the bridge. Sometimes there is no specific evidence apart from the source of the request for your belief and your belief in them—i.e. the parent/child or the husband/wife relationship when the words "I love you" are expressed. It is solely the choice of the individual.

Is this true about the Bible's repeated command to believe for salvation? Dr. Vance presumes that it is. The very existence of such commands in Scripture logically must imply the ability of man to believe the gospel in the same manner as he or she believes anything else. It is a flawed assumption, as will be explained.

The second type of verse that Dr. Vance cites are the verses which imply that there is the possibility of doing so (believing). He offers Luke 8:12 to demonstrate this type of verse.

> Luke 8:12 Those by the way side are they that hear; then cometh the devil, and taketh away the word out of their hearts, <u>lest they should believe and be saved</u>.

Another verse he could have cited is Acts 28:27:

> Acts 28:27 For the heart of this people is waxed gross, and their ears are dull of hearing, and their eyes have they closed; <u>lest they should see</u> with their eyes, <u>and hear</u> with their ears,

<u>and understand with their heart</u>, and should be converted, and I should heal them.

Dr. Vance writes, "If there exists even the slightest possibility that a man could believe, the doctrine of total depravity falls by the wayside."[32] While Luke 8:12 and Acts 28:27 above seem to clearly indicate the possibility that men might believe of their own accord and gain salvation, the point these verses make is that God denies any such possibility for the very reason that He will not allow man to be saved in this manner. If God denies a possibility, then it becomes an impossibility. The heart of fallen man cannot generate saving belief.

In the Luke passage about the four soils, God allows Satan to be the instrument that denies man of any possibility of believing in his heart, apart from His decree. I can hear an attentive Arminian countering with, "What about the seed that sprouted and produced fruit?"

> Luke 8:15 But that on the good ground are they, which in an honest and good heart, having heard the word, keep it, and bring forth fruit with patience.

To this I would ask in rebuttal, when, where, and how did those with an "honest and good heart" get such a heart? Additionally, why did those of the other three "soils," not have such a heart? As mentioned earlier, the Bible does not present a pretty picture of the hearts of natural men. The Luke parable does not tell us where the "honest and good hearts" came from. It only tells us what the seed of the Word does in such "good ground" hearts. The shepherd David was acknowledged as having a heart after God.

> I Sam. 13:14 But now thy kingdom shall not continue: the Lord hath sought him <u>a man after his own heart</u>, and the Lord

---

32 Vance, 238.

hath commanded him to be captain over his people, because thou hast not kept that which the Lord commanded thee.

Where did David get such a heart? Was it his accomplishment? If it was, then David would have something to boast about. I believe that God created this heart in David for His (God's) own purpose. God is the creator of all such hearts by the quickening work of the Holy Spirit at God's ordained time.

This raises the next question: Why, then, do not all men have such hearts? In the Acts passage, God uses men's hardened heart as the obstacle that prevents belief through the senses of sight and hearing alone. Furthermore, John quotes Isaiah, who tells us that it is God that ordains the blinding of the hearts, eyes, and understanding to prevent any "healing."

> John 12:39 Therefore they could not believe, because that Esaias said again,

> John 12:40 <u>He hath blinded</u> their eyes, <u>and hardened their heart</u>; that they should not see with their eyes, nor understand with their heart, and be converted, and I should heal them.

It is God's will that denies any possibility of man believing solely by an act of his own will, just as surely as it was when He denied Adam (mankind) re-entry into the Garden to have physical access to the Tree of Life. Thus, both the possibility of free will heart belief and the re-entry into the garden of Eden were rendered impossible by God.

It was never God's will that caused man (in Adam) to choose to disbelieve and disobey. As Zanchius affirmed in his Position 5, God allows sin, but He does not cause it.[33] Perhaps, regarding the belief or disbelief abilities of man, it is more accurate to say

---

33 Zanchius, 75-76.

that natural man is consistently willing and able to disbelieve the gospel. Therefore, the verses that seem to suggest the possibility of free will belief are actually describing a God ordained impossibility. These truths may strain our powers of logic, but we must not forget the truth of this verse of Isaiah:

> Isa. 55:8 For my thoughts are not your thoughts, neither are your ways my ways, saith the Lord.

**A Cynical Conclusion by Dr. Vance**

Before I bring my critique of Dr. Vance's attempt to discredit the theology of the total sovereignty of God in salvation (Calvinism) to a conclusion, I will offer one final example of where he errs in his theology. In his assault of Calvinism's doctrine proposition of Total Depravity, Dr. Vance offers the following fatalistic, dismissive argument:

> "So if total depravity is true, there is nothing anyone can do except claim Lamentations 3:26 as his life verse:
>
> Lam. 3:26 It is good that a man should both hope and quietly wait for the salvation of the LORD."[34]

Dr. Vance disregards the context of this verse, which is Jeremiah's prophecy to Israel about waiting for their promised salvation and savior. He wrests this verse out of its context by applying it to any man and his salvation. He is cynically implying that, if predestination is true, then the best chance lost men have is for a "hope so" salvation. Lam. 3:26 is a verse that contextually applies to Israel. Israel was prophetically informed about a coming Messiah. As such, they were exhorted to look for and to wait for His promised salvation. In the Gospel of Luke, we are told of two such people, Simeon and Anna, who were doing just that.

---

34 Vance, 190.

Luke 2:25 And, behold, there was a man in Jerusalem, whose name was <u>Simeon</u>; and the same man was just and devout, **waiting for the consolation of Israel**: and the Holy Ghost was upon him.

Luke 2:36 And <u>there was one Anna, a prophetess</u>, the daughter of Phanuel, of the tribe of Asher: she was of a great age, and had lived with an husband seven years from her virginity;

Luke 2:37 And she was a widow of about fourscore and four years, which departed not from the temple, but served God with fastings and prayers night and day.

Luke 2:38 And she coming in that instant gave thanks likewise unto the Lord, and **spake of him to all them that looked for redemption in Jerusalem**.

Apart from the contextual error, Dr. Vance's hypothetical "anyone," as quoted above, must be a lost man, an unbeliever, because believers do not have to wait for their salvation. The other half of the problem with his dismissive conclusion is that natural (lost) men do not, as a rule, choose "life verses" for themselves. Even if they should choose a "life verse," they, by their nature, are not concerned about the salvation that is being waited for in this verse. Dr. Vance likes Lamentation 3:26. He repeats this verse six times in his book to make his cynical assaults on Calvinism. To this quote, I reply with the following rejoinder to Dr. Vance and all who advocate for the free will of man in the miracle of salvation. If it is true that no one's salvation can be accomplished apart from man's free will part in the decision to believe, then somewhere in Scripture, preferably Lamentations, God should have issued this similar, modified lament that echoes the tone of Lam. 3:26. It would read something like this:

> After all that I, the Lord, have done for the salvation of man, all that I, the Lord, can do is hope and quietly wait for the decision of every man's free will in regard to the offer of salvation made to him.

As passionately as the Lord wants to redeem the jewel of His creation, man, whom Satan was allowed to steal, the doctrine of free will mandates that God was, by definition, left to be dependent upon every man's decision to accept salvation and return to the relationship with God as He originally created it to be. Although His choice of the elect was made before time began, Arminian doctrine says salvation is still dependent upon man's choice. In the context of eternity, to be consistent, free will theology must assert that it is God, not man, who is saddled with the "hoping and waiting" of Lam. 3:26 as the best that He can do.

CHAPTER 5

# The Limits, Implications, and Hearing Ability of Man's Will

IT IS WORTH NOTING, that men never object to Scripture's command to "believe" by saying "we can't do this." Whatever men do, it involves a decision of their will. Sure, some will protest by saying that they have occasionally done certain things "against their will." But, I agree with Jonathan Edwards, who postulated that every action taken by man is always in response to the strongest motivating factor of the will that is present at the moment of decision.[35] Thus, while a man may argue that he has done things against his will, such as giving all of the money in his wallet to a stranger on the street who was holding him at

---

35 Edwards, 14.

gunpoint, this would still be an act of his will which responded to the stronger motivation: his life as opposed to his money. This man still chose the option of the strongest influence.

**The Limits of the Will**

Dr. Vance's conclusions about the Bible verses that contain the belief commands and belief possibilities by men, cited in the previous chapter, have some serious problems. First, God has commanded obedience of men, who, in pride, think they can obey. Here are two verses, one from the prophet Jeremiah and one from Jesus, that indicate an inability of men's will because of their nature. The prophet Jeremiah, prophesying against the pride and iniquity of Judah, reveals their inability to do the "good" that God requires with the following analogy:

> Jer. 13:23 Can the Ethiopian change his skin, or the leopard his spots? then <u>may ye also do good, that are accustomed to do evil.</u>

This analogy was God's way of telling Judah that their "doing good" to a level that was acceptable in God's eye was beyond their capability. This inability was not unique to, or confined to, just Judah. It is the condition of all fallen men. Otherwise, Christ did not have to die for all men; just the ones who couldn't change their own "sin spots." Jesus speaks in another verse that points to man's weakness:

> Matt. 26:41 Watch and pray, that ye enter not into temptation: <u>the spirit indeed is willing, but the flesh is weak.</u>

Jesus knows the power that the flesh exerts upon men, even upon those who were committed to Him.

Below is another command from the mouth of Jesus. Yet it is a command that no man has ever met, or ever will meet. Believers, in the dispensation of the law could not meet it. Believers in this age of grace cannot perfectly obey it. Yet, He commands it.

> Matt. 22:37 Jesus said unto him, Thou shalt love the Lord thy God with **all** thy heart, and with **all** thy soul, and with **all** thy mind.

That little word "all" sets the standard that no man can meet.

This is the same Jesus who told his disciples that, without Him, they could do nothing.

> John 15:5 I am the vine, ye are the branches: He that abideth in me, and I in him, the same bringeth forth much fruit: for <u>without me ye can do nothing.</u>

It might be objected that this verse only applies to abiding and bearing fruit. To this I reply that it is disrespectful to believe that the "nothing" Jesus spoke of does not include man's believing for salvation. The "nothing" in this verse is obviously used in the context of spiritual value. We know that man does not control his own physical birth, yet why do so many yet presume that they can, and must, control their own spiritual rebirth? Being saved is an event that has to precede any bearing of fruit. If this verse only applies to fruit bearing, then Jesus' use of the all-inclusive word "nothing" is inaccurate and misleading.

I challenge the Arminian assertion that God never orders man to obey a command which he cannot do. I grant that God does give commands to men that they think they can do, but which He knows they cannot do. Why then would God give such commands? By showing man the standard or level of obedience He requires, God also exposes the inability of pleasing Him through free will obedience and, in turn, exposes man's need for grace.

When God, by His sovereign, pre-creation choice and decree, opens the hearts of His elect, they immediately realize their predicament, and they are irresistibly enabled to accept their Savior by the quickening work of the Holy Spirit. Another term for this is "conviction," and it is the Lord who causes this. The miracle of "irresistible" enabling, or conviction, is the work of the Holy

Spirit, who supernaturally changes the desires of a lost man's heart; in lost men who are His elect. With a new desire implanted in an enabled, opened, new heart, the will of the lost man now chooses to believe the offer of salvation in Christ. He is instantly transformed from a lost sinner to a new creation in Christ. He has just been saved by God's grace.

As their "own gods" (Gen. 3:5), lost men believe that they can meet God's demands by their own efforts. The law (that is, any of God's commands) is the mechanism by which sin is defined. It is actually the barrier for all who think they can obey their way into heaven. Disobedience to any command of God is sin. Paul expressed this very attribute of God's law in his letter to the Romans:

> Rom. 7:7 What shall we say then? Is the law sin? God forbid. Nay, <u>I had not known sin, but by the law</u>: for I had not known lust, except the law had said, Thou shalt not covet.

Dr. Vance, by applying Arminian free will logic to all men, erroneously concludes from all of the Bible verses that command belief, that men possess the ability to believe, apart from any help from God.

It is the vital step of how and why saving belief occurs that is the crux of the issue. Scripture eventually tells us that it can only be done by a gift given to each man by God's grace. There is a scene in Jesus' earthly ministry that hints at man's inability to do this. In Mark's Gospel, a man with a demon-possessed son appeals to Jesus for healing. Jesus asks him a question about his belief. The man gives an honest answer to Jesus about his concern about the level of his own belief.

> Mark 9:23 Jesus said unto him,<u> If thou canst believe</u>, all things are possible to him that believeth.

## THE LIMITS, IMPLICATIONS, AND HEARING ABILITY OF MAN'S WILL

> Mark 9:24 And straightway the father of the child cried out, and said with tears, <u>Lord, I believe; help thou mine unbelief.</u>

This man, honestly and openly before Jesus, admits to his doubts about the adequacy of his own faith. His predicament, with regard to saving faith, is the same for all men. Deep down, in every man who believes that it is his own "free will" faith that will save him, there must be an uncertainty about the sufficiency of their own faith. Without help (the gift of saving faith (Eph. 2:8–9), whatever level of self-generated faith one may have, it is unable to obtain salvation.

Based on the verses he cites, Dr. Vance's conclusion about man's ability to believe is an example of where man's logic has been allowed to supersede God's logic. Again, although God has created and blessed man with the powers of logic, it does not mean that God's ways (and logic) must conform to our ways (and logic). If the whole Word of God is heeded, it tells us that only God's heart-opening grace, delivered through the Holy Spirit, can provide man access to salvation. Man's helplessness to achieve his own salvation by obedience is exposed when all of Scripture is put in the proper context.

### Implications of Having a Free Will

Another serious problem with Dr. Vance's analysis and critique of the doctrine of God's sovereignty, loosely labeled as Calvinism by most of Christianity, is that he fails to consider the implications of the logic-based, free will position. Think about the biblical sequence of man's fall into sin, his knowledge of sin, his knowledge of God, and how salvation occurs. How can fallen man get out of his "sin imprisonment"?

### What Scripture Says Fallen Men Know about God

Every man is a creation of God as a descendent of Adam. But the descendants are not the man that God created. In 1 Cor. 15,

Paul expounds about the various "kinds" of living creatures that God created and the truth that each "kind" is physiologically distinctive from other "kinds." Although the passage below is a revelation about the mystery of resurrection, it is also implied that these distinctive "kinds" of flesh cannot produce flesh of another "kind."

> 1 Cor. 15:39 All flesh is not the same flesh: but there is one kind of flesh of men, another flesh of beasts, another of fishes, and another of birds.

An often-overlooked point about the fall of Adam is that Adam was changed in his "kind" of flesh. He (and Eve) were transformed from fleshly bodies fit for eternal life to bodies now consigned to eventual death. In addition to their spiritual separation from God, Adam and Eve and all of their descendants became what Scripture describes as "natural" men. From these natural, but dying bodies of flesh, they could only produce descendants of like flesh ("kind"). Separated from God and physically changed, they were, nevertheless, not ignorant of Him. Romans 1:20 tells us that there will never be any man who can stand before God and truthfully proclaim his ignorance about God.

As a person grows, he or she reaches what theologians call an age of accountability. This is the age where individuals become consciously aware of the concepts of right (good) and wrong (evil), which Scripture confirms are written in men's hearts (Rom. 2:11–15). Who wrote these things in their hearts? Their creator. The only evil that Adam and Eve were aware of was the eating of the Tree of the Knowledge of Good and Evil. When the serpent (Satan) persuaded them otherwise, the scope of evil was enlarged to them. Their hearts were now in the grip of the desire to please themselves ahead of God's commands to them. This was the promised consequence of eating of the Tree of the Knowledge of Good and Evil. Even before a person becomes conscious of God, their behavior in infancy reveals their fallen nature. There has never been such a thing as an unselfish infant. Babies, by nature, want their way in all things—eating, sleeping, playing, etc. But Paul also tells us that men know what good is by the conviction that arises in their hearts because God has put it there. Man may have been separated from God, but the concepts of good and evil are inherent in all men. Paul writes,

> Rom. 2:11 For there is <u>no respect of persons with God</u>.

> Rom. 2:12 For as many as have sinned without law (Gentiles) shall also perish without law: and as many as have sinned in the law (Jews) shall be judged by the law;

> Rom. 2:13 (For not the hearers of the law are just before God, but the doers of the law shall be justified.

> Rom. 2:14 For when <u>the Gentiles</u>, which have not the law, <u>do by nature the things contained in the law</u>, these, having not the law, <u>are a law unto themselves</u>.

> Rom. 2:15 Which <u>shew the work of the law written in their hearts, their conscience also bearing witness, and their thoughts the mean while accusing or else excusing one another</u>.

In Romans, Paul also tells us that all men are consciously exposed to the general call of God through an awareness of His creation. Therefore, all men are internally made aware of the existence of their creator along with the concepts of right and wrong as the Creator defines them. They will have no excuse when they stand before Him.

> Rom. 1:19 Because <u>that which may be known of God **is manifest in them;** for **God hath shewed it unto them**</u>.

> Rom. 1:20 <u>For the invisible things of him from the creation of the world are clearly seen, being understood by the things that are made, even his eternal power and Godhead;</u> **so that they are without excuse**.

So, Romans 2:15 confirms that, internally and inherently, men know good and evil, while Romans 1:19–20 confirms that men know of the existence of a creator God—not merely by creation around them, but by the understanding of the "invisible things of him." This is a profound truth hidden in this passage that many Christians overlook. It begs the question: When was it possible that all men knew these things? I see only one answer—in the garden, "in Adam." Because of the two truths of these passages, men are without excuse before God. No man will be able to claim ignorance about the reality of, and existence of, God when they stand before Him in judgement, as all men will do, whether they believe it or not.

> Rom. 14:7 For none of us liveth to himself, and no man dieth to himself.

> Rom. 14:8 For whether we live, we live unto the Lord; and whether we die, we die unto the Lord: whether we live therefore, or die, we are the Lord's.

> Rom. 14:9 For to this end Christ both died, and rose, and revived, that he might be Lord both of the dead and living.

Because of this inherent awareness, all men were forever held responsible to seek and search, to find, to know, and to yield in obedience to this God of creation, of whom they were made aware—"in Adam!"

However, the general call of God, which is the display of grace through His creation, coupled with the internal awareness of God through the faculty of conscience, is a grace of God that is demonstrably resistible by men. Men can (and do) write off the creation around them a just a cosmic coincidence. They also can (and do) ignore the inward pull of some sort of internal morality that designates some things as good and other things as evil. Yet, despite the marvel of the creation around them and their own conscious moral awareness, men continually create other gods to worship, and they will be judged for it.

Regardless of gender, culture, race or ethnicity, how can the proclivity of all humans to acknowledge some object, power, or force that is higher in power than themselves be explained? This is what separates man from all other living organisms. Men persist through their own scientific discoveries to produce their own explanations for the creation in which they exist. They also persist through their own man-made religious imaginations to construct their own explanations for whatever sense of higher power they have. In short, men continually demonstrate that both the internal awareness of God and external general call of God's grace are clearly resistible. The tug of conscience and the call of creation can both be ignored. Scripture confirms that all men know God exists. How do they learn what they need for salvation?

**What Scripture Says Fallen Men Need to Know about God**

Right out of the gate (or should I say "Garden"), man stumbled and fell from doing his God-assigned duty.

> Eccl. 12:13 Let us hear the conclusion of the whole matter: Fear God, and keep his commandments: for <u>this is the whole duty of man</u>.

> Eccl, 12:14 <u>For God shall bring every work into judgment, with every secret thing, whether it be good, or whether it be evil</u>.

To seek, to know, and to obey the true God, men need to somehow hear what the Creator has to say to them. The whole history of mankind, from the Genesis account up to the fall of Israel and the destruction of the temple in 70 AD, serves as a demonstration by God that any and all of man's attempts to satisfy God by their independent efforts of obedience for salvation are futile. Now, in the dispensation of grace, the gospel of grace teaches a new path of salvation, which is by grace through a new command—to believe by faith alone in Christ.

> Rom. 10:9 That if thou shalt confess with thy mouth the Lord Jesus, and shalt <u>believe in thine heart</u> that God hath raised him from the dead, thou shalt be saved.

But, in this verse, as in John 3:16, only the benefit of belief is revealed. Neither John 3:16 nor Rom. 10:9 tells us how or why anyone believes. In the age of grace, the law to be obeyed for salvation has been reduced to one simple command. Lost men who hear this requirement of belief naturally think they can do it if they choose to, because, as previously proved, belief is an act men perform (do) on a daily basis. However, many Christians believe that this new, simple command is something they accomplished by an act of their own will and the result was their salvation. Thus, the grace of God in their salvation must be diminished by at least the degree of their contribution to their salvation—their free will choice to believe.

**Lost Man Needs a Hearing Aid—The "How" of Belief**

Paul proceeds in Romans 10 to tell men how faith must come. Men still see no obstacle to their meeting this command. A deeper look at this verse will challenge their conclusion.

> Rom. 10:17 So then <u>faith cometh by hearing, and hearing by the word of God</u>.

The two "hearings" cited in this verse warrant careful consideration. The question should be asked: "How do men hear the word of God?"

There are three processes by which this "hearing" can happen today. First, men can physically read from a Bible, which is the Word of God. By this process, they internally hear the Word in their mind as received through their eyes. Second, they can be told and taught what God's Word says by a preacher, a teacher, or just another believer. This involves processing external, physical sound which then enters the mind.

For those people in the world who, for any reason, lack access to the printed or preached Word of God, there is a third process of hearing "by the word of God." God can speak directly to those He chooses through a dream or a vision. Many Muslim converts to Christianity who have come to believe the gospel testify that this third process is exactly how God reached them. God uses this means of communication with many Muslims because possessing a Bible or listening to any biblical preaching is an offense punishable by death according to the laws of Islam. Thankfully for them, or any such person on earth who has no access to a Bible, God is not prevented from reaching "whom he will" through such dreams and visions.

However, there is a fourth process of hearing that God must combine with one of the three previous types of hearing, if salvation is to occur. It is the process, as Romans 10:17 states it: "hearing by the Word of God." This is the critical required way of hearing that leads to salvation. Note carefully that Romans 10:17 does not say hearing "of" the Word of God. Millions of men have heard the word of God by sight and/or sound. The hearing "by" the word of God is the only "hearing" that can impart saving faith. This type of hearing would be appropriately labeled as "effectual hearing," because this hearing accomplishes God's purpose of salvation in the hearer.

This fourth process of hearing occurs in the heart so that the requirement of belief "in the heart" of Romans 10:9 is met. This is often accomplished, at God's ordained time, through one of the first two processes of hearing—by reading God's Word (through sight) or by hearing God's Word spoken by others (through sound). The essential point to know about these first two processes is that "heart hearing" (the fourth process) does not automatically follow them. Physical hearing alone (by sight or sound) does not assure heart hearing. If the "hearing" of Romans 10:17 only meant mere physical hearing, then there would be many more people saved. Every person who at some time heard the Bible preached or who had the opportunity to read a passage would be saved if physical hearing were the only requirement. The advances of today's technology have enabled widespread Bible reading and hearing possibilities for mankind. But, however many eyes and ears technology can reach with the Bible, only God can reach the heart with it.

Therefore, it becomes God's prerogative as to whether the fourth critical type of "heart hearing" is coupled with either of these first two processes of hearing. Regarding the third process of hearing, by a dream or vision from God, I will dare to suggest that this mode of hearing will always be coupled with the fourth process—heart hearing. I cannot believe that a dream or vision given directly from God will fail in its purpose. Nevertheless, the truth remains that only God can open a heart to "hear."

Reasoning from the context of free will doctrine, to be fair, it must be asserted that every man will become the recipient of the fourth process of hearing the gospel call (heart hearing) that follows one of the first three ways of hearing, so that they can be fairly judged, should they refuse such a call by their "free will." Because the first two types of hearing do not and cannot guarantee the hearing that Romans 10:17 requires, free will doctrine would have to conclude that, if the physical occasion is denied any man to read or hear what the Bible has to say, then God must give at least one visionary call to every person who otherwise lacks any form of Bible access. If "heart" hearing is necessary for salvation, then Arminianism must suppose that it happens for every person so that every person, in their lifetime, will be made responsible. Since Arminian (free will) doctrine denies the place of man's accountability as being found "in Adam," then it is logical to require of God, at some other point, that every person be made accountable for their belief or unbelief, so that any punishment for sin can be justly given to any unbeliever. But this is a doctrinal supposition that strains credibility.

This would partially explain the general Arminian opposition to the doctrine of original sin. To be consistent, they must deny the incorporation of Adam's sin to make all men accountable in order to preserve the sinless innocence of infants until they can make their own accountable decision after having their hearts opened. But Scripture presents a real obstacle to this reasoning. These verses make a clear assertion that Adam's sin was the sin of all men:

> Rom. 5:12 Wherefore, as <u>by one man sin entered into the world, and death by sin; and so death passed upon all men, for that all have sinned</u>.

> 1 Cor. 15:21 For since <u>by man came death</u>, by man came also the resurrection of the dead.

> 1 Cor. 15:22 For as <u>in Adam all die</u>, even so in Christ shall all be made alive.

Because God, in the Garden, pronounced death as the penalty for sin in the Garden, it would be unjust of God for "all" to die in Adam if Adam's sin was not equally ours. A major problem that Dr. Vance and his Arminian brethren face is that they must create some other occasion for the sin of unbelief to occur in every man. If Adam's sin, performed in full awareness of God's command, was not also the sin of every man, then Arminians have to postulate another scenario whereby every man can be justly judged for committing the unforgivable sin of unbelief. To be justly condemned, a man must be fairly aware and fully able to have rejected the gospel. The doctrine of a free will creates this scenario. This is the logic applied by Arminian theology that undergirds the doctrine of man's free will.

Effectual, faith-creating "hearing" must occur beyond mere physical hearing in the mind. It must occur in the heart of man. It is only spiritual hearing in the heart that can produce faith. It is only the Holy Spirit who can open and regenerate the hardened, dark hearts of lost men to the heart hearing of Rom. 10:9. The yet deeper truth, which is denied by free will advocates, is that such heart-hearing work of the Spirit is only performed in those people for whom it was ordained from the beginning of creation by the Father. This will be addressed in Chapter 9.

CHAPTER 6

# The Will - Free or Not So Free? That Is the Question

I NOW TURN TO an examination of the history and logic that drives the Free Will argument. The essence of the argument is the position that subscribes to the free will of man in everything he does, including his decision to believe and be saved. Since the phrase "free will" appears nowhere in the more accurate translations of Scripture, it would be helpful to search for just where in the biblical narrative that the "free will" doctrine might have originated from in Scripture. I believe that men draw it from the Genesis account of Adam's creation and interaction with his Creator. This is where the "image of God" concept is introduced.

**The Image Problem**

We are told in Genesis 1 that man was created by a consensus of the Godhead. Man was to be made in their image (verse 26) and in His image (verse 27). There is no contradiction arising from the plural and singular tenses used in these two verses because of the perfect unity and mystery of the Trinity. Their image and His image are one. After creating man, God then proceeded, in His authority as the creator, to give to man commands to obey in his assigned place in the creation (verses 28–30). This act of creation was performed on the sixth day of creation and it was all seen by God as being very good (verse 31).

> Gen. 1:26 And God said, <u>Let us make man in our image, after our likeness</u>: and let them have dominion over the fish of the sea, and over the fowl of the air, and over the cattle, and over all the earth, and over every creeping thing that creepeth upon the earth.

> Gen. 1:27 <u>So God created man in his own image, in the image of God created he him</u>; male and female created he them.

> Gen. 1:28 And God blessed them, and God said unto them, <u>Be fruitful, and multiply</u>, and <u>replenish</u> the earth, and <u>subdue</u> it: and <u>have dominion</u> over the fish of the sea, and over the fowl of the air, and over every living thing that moveth upon the earth.

> Gen. 1:29 And God said, Behold, I have given you every herb bearing seed, which is upon the face of all the earth, and <u>every tree, in the which is the fruit of a tree yielding seed; to you it shall be for meat</u>.

> Gen. 1:30 And to every beast of the earth, and to every fowl of the air, and to every thing that creepeth upon the earth,

wherein there is life, I have given every green herb for meat: and it was so.

Gen. 1:31 And God saw every thing that he had made, and, behold, it was very good. And the evening and the morning were the sixth day.

I believe that it is from this portion of the creation account that much of Christendom has constructed a flawed view of man's image. Men have logically concluded from verse 26 and 27, and from their own personal experience of a lifetime of making physical and moral decisions, that part of their image, as given by God to Adam and passed on to us, consists of a "free" will with which all decisions are made. I propose that there are two crucial errors in this logic.

**The Wills of Adam and Eve—One of a Kind**

Part of the divine image that God created in man is that of a will. However, there is a profound difference between God's will and man's. From the website Dictionary.com, we find the following definition of the word "will": "the power of the control the mind has over its own actions." How then, do I call the wills of Adam and Eve "one of a kind"? I suggest two aspects that differentiates their wills—one from God's will and the other from the wills of all of their posterity.

**God's Will Contrasted with the Wills of Adam and Eve**

The first aspect is how God's will differs from those of Adam and Eve. God is absolutely free to do whatever He wills to do, but His freedom of will is distinct from man's created will. God can never choose to sin, whereas Adam and Eve possessed an unbiased ability to either obey or disobey what was commanded of them. Because God is His own authority, the exercise of His will is free within the confines of His nature. Similarly, man's will must operate with the limits of his nature; a nature that clearly differs from God's, since God has no commanding authority above Him.

In contrast, man, as a creation of God, was created to be under God's authority. Therefore, there is a possibility that the sin of disobedience existed with Adam and Eve as they were created, but it never existed with God. God would cease to be God if He could sin. Man, by contrast, had to have the freedom to choose obedience or disobedience, otherwise he would have been merely a robot. This facet of man's will is not, and could not be, part of God's image. The biblical truth about the image of man created in the image of God has been erroneously applied in this context. I think this is a pertinent and widely overlooked point in understanding the difference between the wills of God and man.

A further implication about this difference comes from the incarnation of God—Jesus Christ. There is a profound theological question that men continue to wrestle with concerning the humanity of Christ. The question is, could Jesus have ever yielded to Satan's temptations of Him? Simply put, could Jesus have ever sinned? This pulls the debate into the realm of a truly incomprehensible truth of Jesus being simultaneously, fully God and fully man. But this question can have only one answer. Scripture speaks to it:

> Heb. 4:15 For we have not an high priest which cannot be touched with the feeling of our infirmities; but was <u>in all points tempted like as we are, yet without sin.</u>

Those who contend that sin was a possibility like to quote this verse, while maintaining that Jesus could have sinned, but He did not. They argue that if Jesus could not have sinned then the temptations were meaningless. This appeals to logic, but temptations and sin are two different things. Temptation may be strong and tortuous to the soul, but it does not always lead to sin. I oppose this proposition and contend that, being fully God, Jesus could not have sinned. His being tempted in "all points tempted like as we are, yet not sin" (Heb 4:15), is a revelation of the truth of His full deity and His full humanity.

Unlike all men, Jesus was not born under the sin inheritance from Adam. Inherited sin is passed through a father to his posterity, not through the mother. (Exo. 20:5)

> Exo. 20:5 Thou shalt not bow down thyself to them, nor serve them; for I the LORD they God am a jealous God, <u>visiting the iniquity of the fathers upon the children unto the third and fourth generation of them that hate me</u>;

While Satan succeeded in tempting a sinless Adam and Eve, his efforts failed against Jesus because he was tempting God. This testifies to the level of arrogance and rebellion of Satan in thinking that Jesus might yield to him while He (Jesus) was incarnate. A God who could sin could not be God.

Turning to Adam and Eve, it is generally understood that when God gave commands to them, they possessed not only the freedom and ability to obey, but also the freedom and ability to disobey. They were not "robots," compelled to obey, nor were they in bondage to a sinful nature that desired disobedience. It is very important to understand, however, that in their freedom to disobey, Adam and Eve possessed no predisposition to do so. They could never have been pronounced by God as being "good" creations if they had been created with any disposition toward sin. They were totally unbiased toward either choice.

One might think that they should have been biased toward obedience because of their direct relationship with their creator and the perfect creation into which they were placed. But it must be remembered that they had nothing to compare their newly created environment with, so their appreciation of their blessed circumstance would have been limited in that regard. With regard to disobedience, what they had was the freedom to do so.

But the point to be re-emphasized here is that they had no inherent inclination either to do so or to not do so. They were simply allowed the freedom to choose. If ever there was anyone who truly had a free will, it was Adam and Eve, as God created them. Their wills were "one of a kind." This is the only time in all of creation where the free will, of the type that Arminian logic demands of all men, existed.

**Why "All Men"?**

The point that escapes most theologians is the fact that it was this state of free will that Adam (and all men *in Adam*) possessed that made all men responsible for sin. It is why Romans 3:23 also makes the following correct statement about the universal "all" of men.

> Rom. 3:23 For <u>all have sinned</u>, and come short of the glory of God;

If Adam and Eve's descendants are only guilty because of Adam and Eve's sin, Romans 3:23 should read, "Because of Adam and Eve's sin, all are guilty and come short of the glory of God." But, it doesn't. The words of Romans 3:23 are clear. Their sin is our sin, and it includes all humans, even seemingly innocent infants, born or unborn. There is a compound truth to be remembered. It was "in Adam" that all men had both their free will moment and their decision to step into sin. It is a critical error of Free Will doctrine to not recognize when "all men" first sinned and what they lost as a result - their "free will."

In chapter 2 of Genesis, God gives Adam the first "shalt not" command, which Satan chose as his point of attack. It was a command against disobedience and it came with a promised consequence.

> Gen. 2:16 And the Lord God commanded the man, saying, Of every tree of the garden thou mayest freely eat.

> Gen. 2:17 But <u>of the tree of the knowledge of good and evil, **thou shalt not** eat of it: for in the day that thou eatest thereof thou shalt surely die.</u>

Chapter 3 of Genesis then tells us that God allowed Satan to propose disobedience to Adam and Eve, as well as the freedom to persuade them to choose this option, by distorting God's word to them. We know from the account of Satan's tortures inflicted upon Job, that Satan cannot do anything to man apart from God's permission. Therefore, I feel confident to postulate that Satan must have had a similar conversation with God, prior to his Garden of Eden encounter with Adam and Eve. When Satan successfully deceived Adam and Eve, the curse, as described in Genesis 3, passed upon them and upon all of creation.

## The Created Will of Man Contrasted with the Fallen Will of Man

The second differentiating aspect about the wills of Adam and Eve is the result of the profound change they underwent the moment they sinned in the garden. It is a change which I believe many, if not most, Christians overlook. Free Will doctrine simply believes that the unique free will ability, given to Adam and Eve in the Garden of Eden, was untouched by the fall into sin. It is a natural conclusion that this untouched free will has passed down through all of their posterity. They believe that every man enters life with the same "free will" opportunity and ability that Adam and Eve possessed. They see it as incumbent upon God to allow this if He is to be fair in His judgment of them.

This conclusion creates a problem. If it were true, then, theologically, no infant below the age of accountability should ever die of natural causes, because they are not mentally equipped to make a "free will" decision to believe. The only scriptural reason for death is sin (Rom. 6:23). Therefore, unaccountable infants and young children who cannot commit the fatal, free will sin of unbelief, should never die. But it is a fact that infants do die, in the womb and out of it. Scripture also confirms that sin is in infants at conception.

> Ps. 51:5 Behold, I was shapen in iniquity; and in sin did my mother conceive me.

There are ostensibly a couple of logical reasons for the belief that the free will state of Adam and Eve was passed on to all of their posterity. First, Satan, who is adept at mixing his lies with some truth, created this lie. He had told them what the result would be from eating of the tree of the knowledge of good and evil. This was true. Satan is not incapable of speaking truth. He simply keeps truth interspersed with lies to accomplish his ultimate goal of keeping men under his dominion.

When Adam and Eve yielded to Satan's temptation, they immediately knew that a change had occurred in them as they recognized their condition of nakedness.

> Gen. 3:7 And <u>the eyes of them both were opened, and they knew that they were naked</u>; and they sewed fig leaves together, and made themselves aprons.

This was the first "new thing" they knew after they had sinned. What Satan did not tell them about was the bondage their fallen flesh would be in; a bondage that would bias them toward the evil. They were unaware of the truth of Rom. 6:16.

> Rom. 6:16 Know ye not, that <u>to whom ye yield yourselves servants to obey, his servants ye are to whom ye obey</u>; whether of sin unto death, or of obedience unto righteousness?

This fatal bondage does not mean that men would be totally incapable of doing good deeds.

> Matt. 7:11 <u>If ye then, being evil, know how to give good gifts unto your children,</u> how much more shall your Father which is in heaven give good things to them that ask him?

Arminians love to use such verses as this to prove that men can still choose to do good. But ability of any deed to merit salvation was clearly denied in Romans.

> Rom. 3:20 Therefore by <u>the deeds of the law</u> (the definer of good and evil) <u>there shall no flesh be justified in his sight</u>: for by the law is the knowledge of sin.

Any deed done totally apart from God is a work of man. This would include the false premise about the free will act (deed) of belief. Satan's desired deception is for men to believe in the power of their own wills to decide about God's offer of salvation, while they simultaneously fail to realize the bondage of their wills to fallen natures. If the helplessness of their bondage is not acknowledged, then any urgency for salvation is removed.

Another impediment to a correct understanding of limitation of man's will arises from the biblical truth that tells us that the power of the lusts of the flesh was not removed from men who are saved. Paul defines this truth in Romans 7 when he laments the hold that his flesh has on his own desires. He is aware that there are two opposing forces tugging at his will. This was self-recognized by Paul, who could easily be described by most believers as a "super Christian." No believer can deny the application of this same self-analysis to himself or herself. So the second differentiating aspect between the will of created man and fallen man is the assumption that the descendants of Adam and Eve inherited, and now operate with, the same unbiased "free" will that Adam and Eve were created with.

The Scriptures also seem to provide logical reasons for a belief in free will. The reasons arise from the facts that God, throughout Scripture, continued to give commands and directions to men after the expulsion from the Garden of Eden. The rewards and the punishments that attended His commands were always made contingent upon obedience. Again, this speaks to men's logic. It implies that they must have full ability to comply with any command God would give, because God would not command anything that man could not do. Would He?

To repeat, it is true that God did not command anything of man that he could not do. What was lost in the fall of man was the will (desire) to comply according to God's acceptable standard—which is perfect, heart-driven obedience. After the fall, men were left to make their own judgments about their obedience. It did not take long to demonstrate their desire for their own way, as Cain proved. Satan had tempted our "free will" parents into sin, but thereafter men would begin to yield to their newly acquired sin nature. Outside the Garden of Eden, where men were allowed to live by their conscience alone, the imaginations of their hearts were continually evil (Gen. 6:5). When God's chosen people, Israel, were given the Law as the guide to acceptable obedience, they could not meet God's requirement of perfect obedience, despite their repeated promises to do so. Finally, through Paul, when salvation was offered through faith alone, an even deeper truth had to be revealed by Paul. It was the truth that belief could not occur apart from the revealed mystery of the gift of faith given by God's grace. Neither partial Law obedience nor intellectual belief could obtain salvation. Only heart-generated belief (faith) would suffice and would be acceptable in God's eyes. How could this happen in hearts that continually imagine evil apart from God's gift of faith to His elect? How could belief in the gospel (a spiritual thing) happen in hearts of natural men, who Scripture says are unable to discern spiritual things?

> 1 Cor. 2:14 But the natural man receiveth <u>not the things of the Spirit of God</u>: for they are foolishness unto him: **neither can he know** them, because <u>they are spiritually discerned</u>.

## Summary of the Errors of Logic about Free Will

In summary, I contend that it is from the Genesis account of the creation of man that free will theology draws these critical errors of logic:

1. The belief that the freedom of God's will equates with the freedom of created man's will because of their being made in God's image.
2. The belief that freedom of Adam and Eve's will remained unchanged after they had sinned.
3. The belief that their posterity inherited the same free will capacity to obey (believe) or disobey (disbelieve) that Adam and Eve were created with.
4. The belief that the sin of all men did not originate in Adam by their free will existence "in Adam," as Scripture states. If "in Adam all sinned," then "in Adam" all also had his free will.

CHAPTER 7

# Biblical Perspectives about the Will of Man

**Free Will and the Four States of Man**
THERE ARE SEVERAL CONTEXTUAL aspects that deserve further consideration with regard to the will of believers. First, much of Christendom fails to acknowledge a unique truth about believers while they remain in this life. The essence of this first point is that there has never been a state of "dual-willed" mankind like that of the believers in the dispensation of God's grace. By this I mean that there has never been a spiritual condition of man similar to that of born-again, Holy Spirit indwelt, believers in this age of grace, before they die and meet the Lord in heaven. As noted earlier, Adam was unique in that he was able to sin but had no predisposition to sin. After the fall, Adam and all of his fallen posterity were locked into a nature that willed to serve their individual wills. Even though fallen men could be moved by conscience to do some good deeds, their wills were enslaved

to their fallen nature. As cited earlier, from Adam to Noah, Scripture portrays the sin-driven evolution of men's hearts.

> Gen. 6:5 And God saw that the wickedness of man was great in the earth, and that every imagination of the thoughts of his heart was only evil continually.

In the dispensations of promise and law, when God formed and chose Israel, the Holy Spirit came upon certain men to direct their actions, but it never indwelt them. In the dispensation of the grace of God, (Eph. 3:2 If ye have heard of the dispensation of the grace of God which is given me to you-ward), believers are now sealed with the indwelling Holy Spirit and they are made into new creations of God (2 Cor. 5:17).

> 2 Cor. 5:17 Therefore if any man be in Christ, <u>he is a new creature</u>: old things are passed away; behold, all things are become new.

Yet, while believers remain alive in their fallen bodies with a fallen nature, the two natures now within every believer continue to wage war to control the will (Rom. 7). Paul, God's chosen apostle to the Gentiles, testified to this.

> Rom. 7:21 I find then a law, that, when I would do good, evil is present with me.

> Rom. 7:22 <u>For I delight in the law of God after the inward man:</u>

> Rom. 7:23 <u>But I see another law in my members, warring against the law of my mind, and bringing me into captivity to the law of sin which is in my members.</u>

He then laments this predicament with a rhetorical question in verse 24:

# BIBLICAL PERSPECTIVES ABOUT THE WILL OF MAN

> Rom 7:24 O wretched man that I am! who shall deliver me from the body of this death?

and then supplies the answer in verse 25:

> Rom 7:25 I thank God through Jesus Christ our Lord. So then with the mind I myself serve the law of God; but with the flesh the law of sin.

Today, believers, like Adam, again have the capability to choose, by their will, to obey God or to disobey. However, today's believers, unlike Adam, now have two opposing dispositions within them that produce the war that Paul describes in Rom. 7. I make this assertion about Adam's lack of any predisposition, good or sinful, because, unlike believers saved by God's grace, Adam, as far as we know from Scripture, was not indwelt by the Holy Spirit. God merely laid out His commands to Adam and left him to his own unbiased will to obey or disobey.

Putting it another way, Adam's freedom of will to choose was done in a state of pure innocence. The "new creature" believer of 2 Cor. 5:17 must now make his willful choices in a conflicted state where two natures now pull his will to yield to either the Spirit or the flesh.

But, it must be remembered that every "new creation" believer was created by the Holy Spirit–enabled choice of his or her will to believe. This belief was not accomplished by any unassisted choice of a fallen, captive will. This is plainly supported in John 1.

> John 1:12 But <u>as many as received him</u>, to them gave he power to become the sons of God, even to them that believe on his name:

> John 1:13 Which were born, not of blood, **nor of the will of the flesh, nor of the will of man**, but of God.

Not until believers die and are joined to Christ in heaven will the flesh and its power to induce sin be removed. The dual-willed man will cease to exist. The resurrected believer will be unable to sin and will be totally submitted to the Holy Spirit within him or her. This transformation is foretold in 1 Corinthians:

> 1 Cor. 15:54 So <u>when this corruptible shall have put on incorruption</u>, and this mortal shall have put on immortality, then shall be brought to pass the saying that is written, <u>Death is swallowed up in victory</u>.
>
> 1 Cor. 15:55 O death, where is thy sting? O grave, where is thy victory?
>
> 1 Cor. 15:56 The sting of death is sin; and the strength of sin is the law.

For death to be swallowed up in victory there cannot be any more sin. When one is searching for the correct answer to the question of who makes the first choice in salvation, God or the individual, it is helpful to review the four states of man with regard to the operation of the will. The following table can serve as a helpful contextual reminder when one is trying to correctly understand the changing role of the will in mankind's creation, fall, and redemption.

# BIBLICAL PERSPECTIVES ABOUT THE WILL OF MAN

| Categories of man | Capability of the will to please God | Influencer(s) of the will | State of man's nature |
|---|---|---|---|
| As created by God | Created free to choose obedience or disobedience. | Unbiased self-choice | Pure innocence—a good creation of God. |
| All unbelievers of all ages—fallen and born in sin | Able to choose disobedience. Desires self over God. Able to obey intermittently, but unable to choose saving-faith obedience by one's will. | A fallen conscience in captivity to the desires of the flesh in a world dominated by Satan. | Totally fallen in sin—a captive of Satan—now, by nature, a child of God's wrath. |
| All believers from Gen. 1 through Acts 8 (Believing Jews or Jewish proselytes) | Able to obey God's commands of their day, but without the aid of the Holy Spirit; still under the power of the flesh. (But, if saved, they are yet only unknowingly saved by grace through the gift of faith.) | The commands of God for their day (plus moments of Holy Spirit conviction and/or filling) versus the still active power of the flesh.* | Still old-natured men of God's choosing, but left to struggle in obedience without the indwelling Holy Spirit. |

| Believers who become part of the Body of Christ (a mystery revealed only to Paul) | Enabled to obey and believe by the power of the indwelling of the Holy Spirit, yet still able to sin under the power of the flesh. | The indwelling Holy Spirit in battle with the still-existent power of the flesh. | Now dual-natured men of God's choosing, who are indwelt, sealed, and enabled to obey by the Holy Spirit. |
|---|---|---|---|
| All resurrected believers in heaven | Unable to disobey (sin); desires only to obey and please God. | A new nature with a new will desiring only obedience. | Old sin nature is dead. A new creation with a nature that desires only to love and serve Christ. |

\* Believers influenced by, but not indwelt by the Holy Sprit

**Free Will and Eternal Security**

Consider this next point about free will. There is a question that seldom, if ever, gets asked. The question is this: If it is true that the will, after mankind's fall into sin, remains free and able to freely choose to believe or reject God's gospel that leads to salvation, then does this ability to freely choose or reject continue within every believer? If it does, then the historic doctrine of eternal security of the believer is a deception. If a believer retains his or her power of a free will with regard to this all-important decision of belief, and he or she still lives under the pull and temptations of the flesh, then the power to willfully disbelieve after salvation must be possible. The freedom to return to willful disbelief would mean the loss of salvation.

# BIBLICAL PERSPECTIVES ABOUT THE WILL OF MAN

Believers can (and do) fall into some dire life circumstances that may convince them that God has forgotten them. Can they opt out and return to unbelief? Arminian (free will) doctrine would be hard-pressed to say no. This poses a real danger that Satan may use to induce believers who still theoretically retain the Arminian belief in the power of free will. The danger would be that of returning to the original decision of the will to disbelieve and disobey. So much for "blessed assurance", when one's free will may be turned back to disbelief.

Interestingly, I have never heard or read a free will advocate propose exactly this possibility. Yes, there are certainly Christians who disavow the doctrine of eternal security of the believer. However, they hinge the loss of salvation based upon a certain level (never clearly defined) of sinful behavior. But I have never heard the loss attributed to a mere decision to just disbelieve. But the thinking that argues for free will prior to salvation would be logic bound to allow it after the salvation decision is made. If free will theology does not allow for the loss of free will in the garden, then how could it allow for the loss of free will after salvation? To this theology, free will must be an eternal power.

If this is true, then it is logical to assert that a believer's security of salvation is secure only to the degree that he or she remains in agreement with their decision to believe. In succinct terms, if they are free and able to believe, then they must be free and able to disbelieve. It would be logically inconsistent to say that, after their salvation, God removes, or overrides, their free will. I do not know of any Scripture that confirms this.

Nevertheless, most Arminians do not carry free will doctrine to these logical extremes, yet they cannot explain why they don't. Consider how frightening it would be if believers were left to worry about the free will, that was used to secure salvation, being able to lead them back into unbelief. They would exist at the mercy of external circumstances that might persuade their "free wills" away from belief.

## The Triune Composition of Man

As it relates to the will, it is important to look at what Scripture says about how the spirit of man was affected when he fell into sin and how this event affected his will. In further pursuit of understanding man and the operation of his will, it is helpful to examine man's composition, as God created him. If it is true that man was made in the image of God, but certainly not equal to God, how then is he made? It is clear from the Bible that God is a Trinity, three in one. Correspondingly, God's image in the creation of man consists of three parts—body, soul, and spirit. The body is the part of man by which he experiences God's creation physically. The soul is that part of man that experiences creation emotionally and mentally. The spirit is the part of man whereby he was made to connect with and commune with the creator, God. The Trinity is three parts in one, man is one with three parts.

In the debate about what man can and cannot do by his own will, Scripture makes the point that it was the spirit of man, his direct connection to God, that immediately died with Adam's sin. The sin in the Garden broke Adam's (man's) direct relationship with God. Man's spirit was separated from God's Spirit. There is a truth revealed in 2 Corinthians that proves the existence of this direct relationship. Paul writes about the new commission or ministry that Christ assigns to His body, the church.

> 2 Cor. 5:18 And all things are of God, who hath reconciled us to himself by Jesus Christ, and hath given to us the ministry of reconciliation.

By definition, the word "reconcile" means the restoring of two parties that were previously united. This verse plainly implies that God and man had a prior direct relationship. Many Christian teachers fail to acknowledge that it was not only Adam's spirit that died but the death of all men's spirits also. Theologically, the term death means a separation from God. I re-emphasize that Romans 5 and 1 Cor. 15 make it clear that "death" for all men occurred "in Adam."

> Rom. 5:12 Wherefore, as by one man sin entered into the world, and death by sin; and <u>so death passed upon all men, for that all have sinned</u>.

> 1 Cor. 15:22 For as <u>in Adam all die</u>, even so in Christ shall all be made alive.

Man was not created to die, but death came upon him by his own willful choice. It was not only physical death that Paul wrote about. This sin "in Adam" brought immediate spiritual death (separation) to man. This initial sin also assured a physical death that would happen to all men at some time in their life—an appointed time.

> Heb. 9:27 And as <u>it is appointed unto men once to die</u>, but after this the judgment:

It brought all of mankind into Satan's dominion.

> Eph. 2:2 Wherein in time past <u>ye walked according to the course of this world, according to the prince of the power of the air, the spirit that now worketh in the children of disobedience</u>:

Adam and all men became Satan's slave servants, not hired servants. Man chose his servitude to Satan. Remember:

> Rom. 6:16 Know ye not, that <u>to whom ye yield yourselves servants to obey</u>, his servants ye are to whom ye obey; whether of sin unto death, or of obedience unto righteousness?

Because image and makeup of man consists of three parts, it merits a look at the effect of death on these three parts and how God deals with each part in the context of eternity.

**1. Man's Spirit**

Sin disconnected man's spirit from God so that all men were deemed spiritually dead and assured of a physical death. They were now in need of resurrection—a spiritual resurrection. First, it was Christ's resurrection that provided the opportunity for the spiritual portion of man's spiritual resurrection. This resurrection, or restoration, occurs immediately at the moment of a person's belief in Jesus Christ as their Savior. The fact of spiritual death and spiritual resurrection is made clear by the following verses:

> Eph. 2:1 And <u>you hath he quickened, who were dead in trespasses and sins</u>.

> Eph. 2:5 Even <u>when we were dead in sins, hath quickened us together with Christ</u>, (by grace ye are saved.)

> Eph. 2:6 And hath <u>raised us up together, and made us sit together in heavenly places in Christ Jesus</u>.

> Rom. 7:6 But now we are delivered from the law, <u>that being dead</u> wherein we were held; that we should <u>serve in newness of spirit</u>, and not in the oldness of the letter.

> Col. 2:12 Buried with him in baptism, wherein also <u>ye are risen with him through the faith of the operation of God</u>, who hath raised him from the dead.

> Col. 2:13 And <u>you, being dead in your sins and the uncircumcision of your flesh, hath he quickened together with him, having forgiven you</u>.

The verses above are being addressed to physically living believers about their former "dead" spiritual condition.

What about the spirit of unbelievers? If they never believe, their spirits will never be reconnected to God. In that context, they will remain spiritually dead, disconnected from God eternally.

## 2. Man's Soul

While man's spirit died by his sin in the Garden, lost men continue their life in two compositions—body and soul. When physical death occurs, the believer's body and soul are separated. However, the Bible never says anything about the soul dying or sleeping, as some false doctrines assert. At the death of the body, the souls of men get relocated. Prior to the dispensation of grace, the believer's soul was carried to Abraham's bosom in the region called paradise, or the third heaven by some. In contrast, the soul of the unbeliever departs for an appointed destination also. This destination is called hell in Scripture. Jesus gave the disciples a terrifying glimpse of it in the story (not parable) of Lazarus and the rich man.

> Luke 16:22 And it came to pass, that the beggar died, and was carried by the angels into Abraham's bosom: <u>the rich man also died, and was buried</u>;

> Luke 16:23 <u>And in hell he lift up his eyes, being in torments, and seeth Abraham afar off, and Lazarus in his bosom.</u>

> Luke 16:24 <u>And he cried</u> and said, Father Abraham, have mercy on me, and send Lazarus, that he may dip the tip of his finger in water, and cool my tongue; <u>for I am tormented in this flame.</u>

> Luke 16:25 But Abraham said, Son, remember that thou in thy lifetime receivedst thy good things, and likewise Lazarus evil things: but now he is comforted, <u>and thou art tormented</u>.

Luke 16:26 <u>And beside all this, between us and you there is a great gulf fixed: so that they which would pass from hence to you cannot; neither can they pass to us, that would come from thence.</u>

Here is what we learn about this location of the departed souls from this account in Luke's gospel:
- prior to the resurrection of Christ, there were two real destinations for departed souls—paradise (Abraham's bosom) for believers (Lazarus) and hell for unbelievers (the rich man);
- occupants of each place can see each other;
- there is an impassable gulf between the two sections;
- Hell is a place of unrelenting torment;
- paradise is a place of comfort (in Abraham's bosom);
- Hell is inhabited by departed souls, not bodies;
- the torments of the lost souls are as real as if they still had their bodies.

This separation will not be a quiet one. Think for a moment how the agony of the lost will be not only from the real torments of hell, (for example, the rich man's begging for one drop of water), but also from the added torment of being able to see what they could have had if they had believed. Lost men will experience an eternal state of agony of regret for their lifetime rejection of God and His offered salvation. In the synoptic gospels, there are some vivid descriptions of the torment that awaits the unbelieving. The repeated phrase "weeping and gnashing of teeth," as seen in the verses that follow, express an eternal state of mental, emotional, and physical torment that awaits those who die unsaved.

Matt. 8:12 But the children of the kingdom shall be cast out into outer darkness: <u>there shall be weeping and gnashing of teeth.</u>

> Matt. 22:13 Then said the king to the servants, Bind him hand and foot, and take him away, and cast him into outer darkness; <u>there shall be weeping and gnashing of teeth</u>.

> Matt. 24:51 And shall cut him asunder, and appoint him his portion with the hypocrites: <u>there shall be weeping and gnashing of teeth</u>.

> Matt. 25:30 And cast ye the unprofitable servant into outer darkness: <u>there shall be weeping and gnashing of teeth</u>.

> Luke 13:28 <u>There shall be weeping and gnashing of teeth</u>, when ye shall see Abraham, and Isaac, and Jacob, and all the prophets, in the kingdom of God, and you yourselves thrust out.

The fate of unbelievers is in stark contrast to that which believers receive. We are told the destination of the souls of all who were saved by faith before the resurrection and ascension of Christ. I believe they are "the captivity led captive" of Eph. 8:9, where it is said that Christ descended into the lower parts of the earth. This view could be disputed, but Scripture seems to indicate it.

> Eph. 4:8 Wherefore he saith, When he <u>ascended up on high, he led captivity captive, and gave gifts unto men</u>.

> Eph. 4:9 (Now that he ascended, what is it but that <u>he also descended first into the lower parts of the earth?</u>)

Why did He do this? One purpose was to preach the final gospel truth about the death and resurrection of Jesus Christ to them and then to lead those souls in paradise to His throne "on high." Peter states this in his first epistle:

1 Pet. 4:6 <u>For for this cause was the gospel preached also to them that are dead</u>, that they might be judged according to men in the flesh, but live according to God in the spirit.

Jesus confirmed to them that He was the King and Savior they had waited for. After this relocating of the saints in paradise to heaven, gifts (rewards) were given to all deceased believers in heaven (Eph. 4:8).

Once Christ led this group to heaven, a different destination awaited the souls of believers. In the present dispensation of grace, at physical death, we are told that a believer's soul leaves the body and is directly reunited with Jesus, who is now in heaven, seated at God's right hand.

2 Cor. 5:6 Therefore we are always confident, knowing that, <u>whilst we are at home in the body, we are absent from the Lord</u>:

2 Cor. 5:7 (For we walk by faith, not by sight:)

2 Cor. 5:8 We are confident, I say, and willing rather to be <u>absent from the body, and to be present with the Lord</u>.

The destination for the souls of unbelievers remains unchanged. They will still continue to go to hell in this age, where they await the judgment at the Great White Throne (Rev. 20:11). The horrible truth that bears repeating for unbelievers is that the experiences and sensations of torture for their souls are as real as if they were in an actual physical body and they last forever. This is the truth that all unbelievers either ignore or are willing to gamble is not true.

### 3. Man's Body

Finally, at their physical death, the bodies of both believers and unbelievers go to the grave in some form and sense. The

## BIBLICAL PERSPECTIVES ABOUT THE WILL OF MAN

body of every deceased man, no matter how they died, will be resurrected at God's appointed hour, to one of two distinct destinies as previously discussed and about which the apostle John wrote. Graves contain dead bodies. Regardless of the ultimate fate of the body itself, whether it is lost at sea, is disintegrated by an explosion or cremation, or is buried in normal fashion, all bodies, dead or alive, will be resurrected. No one will escape their judgment by God by any kind of disintegration of their bodies.

> John 5:28 Marvel not at this: for the hour is coming, in the which <u>all that are in the graves shall hear his voice,</u>

Next, the two destinies are clearly defined:

> John 5:29 <u>And shall come forth</u>; <u>they that have done good, unto the resurrection of life</u>; <u>and they that have done evil, unto the resurrection of damnation.</u>

In Scripture, the Greek word for resurrection is *anastasis*. It means "to be raised to life again" or "to stand again." Resurrection is a term that relates to both the body and the spirit. It must be noted that only the believer's spirit will be resurrected or revived to life at their moment of belief, while the bodies of all men will be resurrected as John 5:28–29 just confirmed. The spirit of the lost will remain eternally separated from God.

In God's eyes, there are only two classes of men in the Bible, the lost and the saved. However, in Scripture there are five resurrections that can be correctly discerned. Lost men will have only one resurrection. This happens at the Great White Throne judgment is described in Revelation 20:

> Rev. 20:11 And I saw a great white throne, and him that sat on it, from whose face the earth and the heaven fled away; and there was found no place for them.

Rev. 20:12 And I saw the dead, small and great, stand before God; and the books were opened: and another book was opened, which is the book of life: and the dead were judged out of those things which were written in the books, according to their works.

By contrast, relating to Christ and His saved elect, there is a verse that alludes to four resurrections in 1 Corinthians:

1 Cor. 15:23 But every man in his own order: Christ [1] the firstfruits [2]; afterward they that are Christ's at his coming [3 & 4].

Christ's resurrection (1) is affirmed in Romans 1:

Rom. 1:3 Concerning his Son Jesus Christ our Lord, which was made of the seed of David according to the flesh;

Rom. 1:4 And declared to be the Son of God with power, according to the spirit of holiness, by the resurrection from the dead:

The means of the bodily resurrection of all believers, (2) and (3 & 4) is stated in Romans 8:

Rom. 8:10 And if Christ be in you, the body is dead because of sin; but the Spirit is life because of righteousness.

Rom. 8:11 But if the Spirit of him that raised up Jesus from the dead dwell in you, he that raised up Christ from the dead shall also quicken your mortal bodies by his Spirit that dwelleth in you.

The time of the resurrection of the first fruits (2) of believers, who died before Christ, is noted in Matthew 27:

> Matt. 27:51 And, behold, the veil of the temple was rent in twain from the top to the bottom; and the earth did quake, and the rocks rent.

> Matt. 27:52 And <u>the graves were opened; and many **bodies of the saints which slept arose**</u>,

Regarding those who are Christ's at His coming (3 & 4), there are two "comings." The (3) "coming" was prophesied in Revelation 20 and is called the first resurrection:

> Rev. 20:4 And I saw thrones, and they sat upon them, and judgment was given unto them: and I saw <u>the souls of them that were beheaded for the witness of Jesus, and for the word of God</u>, and which had not worshipped the beast, neither his image, neither had received his mark upon their foreheads, or in their hands; and they lived and reigned with Christ a thousand years.

> Rev. 20:5 But the rest of the dead lived not again until the thousand years were finished. <u>This is the first resurrection</u>.

> Rev. 20:6 <u>Blessed and holy is he that hath part in the first resurrection: on such the second death hath no power, but they shall be priests of God and of Christ, and shall reign with him a thousand years</u>.

The description of this resurrection follows the chapter 19 account of Christ's prophesied return or second coming to earth, where He destroys His enemies and sets up His Kingdom. The "those who are His" of 1 Cor. 15:23, labeled by me as (3) above, are the tribulation saints who will reign with Christ in the millennium.

The other "coming" of Christ (4) was not prophesied, but was later revealed by Jesus through Paul. This is Christ's secret coming for the Church, which is His body. This is the third occasion for the resurrection of believers. Both dead and living church-age believers (4) at this "coming" will be resurrected to new heavenly bodies. It is documented in 1 Thessalonians:

> 1 Thess. 4:16 For the Lord himself shall descend from heaven with a shout, with the voice of the archangel, and with the trump of God: <u>and the dead in Christ shall rise first</u>.

> 1 Thess. 4:17 Then <u>we which are alive and remain shall be caught up together with them</u> in the clouds, to meet the Lord in the air: and so shall we ever be with the Lord.

(Those mentioned in verse 17, who, "are alive and remain" are not technically resurrected, but rather are translated to heaven at the return of Christ in the air for his church, which is his body.)

To summarize the scriptural path and destinies of the three parts of man, it is necessary to remember:

1. Man's connection to God (his spirit) was broken in the Garden of Eden (Rom. 5:12).

> Rom. 5:12 Wherefore, as <u>by one man sin entered into the world</u>, and death by sin; and so death passed upon all men, for that <u>all have sinned</u>.

The spirits of men who are saved are resurrected in the sense that they are revived or quickened back to life. Their connection to God is re-established.

> Eph. 2:5 Even when we were dead in sins, hath quickened us together with Christ, (by grace ye are saved.)

2. Scripture never speaks of the soul of man dying and thus never being resurrected. They are merely relocated, depending upon when they died and whether they died as a believer or unbeliever.

3. The bodies of all men get resurrected. What their bodies are resurrected to depends upon whether they died as a believer or unbeliever.

> John 5:28 Marvel not at this: for the hour is coming, in the which all that are in the graves shall hear his voice,

> John 5:29 And shall come forth; they that have done good, unto the resurrection of life; and they that have done evil, unto the resurrection of damnation.

At the Great White Throne judgment, the already tortured souls of all unsaved men will be reunited with their resurrected bodies fit for an eternity of literal physical suffering when their bodies and souls are cast into the lake of fire, as Jesus foretold in Rev. 20:

> Rev. 20:14 And death and hell were cast into the lake of fire. This is the second death.

> Rev.20:15 And whosoever was not found written in the book of life was cast into the lake of fire.

Mark's gospel account gives us further description of this fire of God's judgment.

> Mark 9:44 Where their worm dieth not, and the fire is not quenched.

The emotional and physical destiny of the unsaved, for eternity, is terrifying to consider.

To supplement the reader's understanding of the scriptural sequencing of men's bodily resurrections, the attached chart by the famous Biblical chartist of the early 1900's, Dr. Clarence Larkin, is offered as a visual aid.[36] Note the four bodily resurrections

---

[36] Illustration by Rev. Clarence Larkin, *Resurrections and Judgments*. Image courtesy of ClarenceLarkinCharts.com.

from "the grave." Notice also from this chart, the five judgments that follow each particular resurrection.

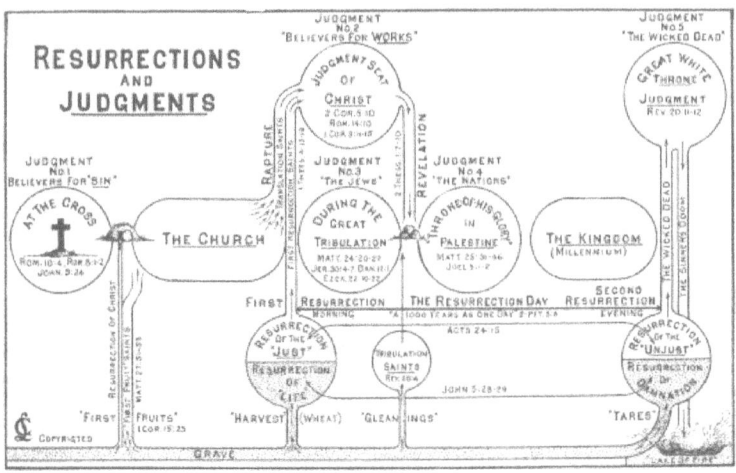

(I will add one critique of Rev. Larkin's chart. Judgment No.1 was the judgement for the sins of all men, not just believers.

> 2 Cor. 5:14 For the love of Christ constraineth us; because we thus judge, <u>that if one died for all, then were all dead</u>.

This was addressed earlier in the futile debate over the atonement and whether it was limited or unlimited

It is critical to understand that in all of the transformations and movements of the three parts of man: spirit, soul, and body, there are only two final outcomes: eternal life or eternal damnation. It is my contention in this book that the Bible presents the truth that the will of man was solely responsible for the condemnation of all men and that it was God's will, according to His eternal purpose, to bring "whomsoever He willed" to eternal life. Only God can create the will and nature of man. Only God can recreate the will and nature of "whomsoever He wills."

**Unable? Unwilling? Or Both?**

## BIBLICAL PERSPECTIVES ABOUT THE WILL OF MAN

It is undeniable that the will of man, after Adam, was now corrupted. All men became "as Gods," knowing good and evil (Gen 3:5) from eating of the forbidden tree. Corrupted nature and man-centered logic became the main drivers of the wills after the fall of men into sin.

> Gen. 3:5 For God doth know that in the day ye eat thereof, then your eyes shall be opened, and <u>ye shall be as gods, knowing good and evil</u>.

Man was physically and mentally able to obey, but his new fallen nature, inherited from Adam, made it impossible to please God by the standard He requires—perfect, willing obedience from the heart. By the new fallen nature, "self" assumed priority over God with regard to obedience. He was spiritually unable to perfectly obey, but Scripture did not allow for anything less. God's law required it, but men, under the law, could not do it. By their fallen wills, they did not want to do it. If the standard for law keeping was expressed in a sports parlance, it would be said that, to be saved, a person must pitch a perfect game (baseball) or roll a 300 game (bowling). Here is the standard that scripture demands:

> Josh. 1:8 This book of the law shall not depart out of thy mouth; but thou shalt meditate therein day and night, that thou mayest observe <u>to do according to **all** that is written therein</u>: for then thou shalt make thy way prosperous, and then thou shalt have good success.

> James 2:10 <u>For whosoever shall keep the whole law, and yet offend in one point, he is guilty of **all**</u>.

Paul confirmed the impossibility of salvation by works (obedience) through the very fact that the Father sent His Son, Jesus Christ, to die, thereby eliminating any possibility of justification by works.

> Rom. 3:28 Therefore we conclude that <u>a man is justified by faith without the deeds of the law</u>.

> Gal. 2:21 I do not frustrate the grace of God: for <u>if righteousness come by the law, then Christ is dead in vain</u>.

The impossibility of justification by works refutes Arminian theology, which believes that Adam's posterity retained the same unbiased ability of the will to choose to obey God as their created parents. Although men can choose to do good works, the fatal deficiency in their capacity to obey was the unwillingness of their fallen nature to believe God for salvation, in their hearts, by their own will. God could not allow a "free will" decision to fix man's sin problem.

Saving belief is a spiritual work. As 1 Cor. 2:14 says about things of the Spirit: "They are foolishness unto him (natural man): <u>neither can he know them, because they are spiritually discerned</u>." Being now spiritually dead toward God and separated from Him, they have a corrupted will (desire), thus no ability to believe for salvation. After their sin in the Garden of Eden, men did not seek God.

> Ps. 14:2 The Lord looked down from heaven upon the children of men, to see <u>if there were any that did understand, and seek God</u>.

> Ps. 14:3 They are <u>all gone aside</u>, they are <u>all together become filthy</u>: there is <u>none that doeth good, no, not one.</u>

Mankind, by their new fallen nature, now had the same attitude about God as the citizenry in the parable of the nobleman.

> Luke 19:12 He said therefore, A certain nobleman went into a far country to receive for himself a kingdom, and to return.

> Luke 19:13 And he called his ten servants, and delivered them ten pounds, and said unto them, Occupy till I come.

> Luke 19:14 But <u>his citizens hated him</u>, and sent a message after him, <u>saying, We will not have this man to reign over us</u>.

## Does Scripture Support Man's Free Will?

Scripture also confirms that God would not allow man to grasp the severity of his lost condition and then, by his own reasoning, understand his need for a Savior. A foreshadowing of this point occurred when the Lord God promptly banned Adam from the Garden of Eden for the reason stated in verse 22.

> Gen. 3:22 And the Lord God said, Behold, the man is become as one of us, to know good and evil: and now, <u>lest he put forth his hand, and take also of the tree of life, and eat, and live for ever:</u>

> Gen. 3:23 Therefore <u>the LORD God sent him forth from the garden of Eden</u>, to till the ground from whence he was taken.

Adam and Eve immediately knew something was wrong and took action.

> Gen. 3:7 And <u>the eyes of them both were opened, and they knew that they were naked</u>; and they sewed fig leaves together, and made themselves aprons.

> Gen. 3:8 And they heard the voice of the LORD God walking in the garden in the cool of the day: and <u>Adam and his wife hid themselves from the presence of the LORD God</u> amongst the trees of the garden.

> Gen. 3:9 And the LORD God called unto Adam, and said unto him, Where art thou?

> Gen. 3:10 And he said, I heard thy voice in the garden, and I was afraid, because I was naked; and I hid myself.

> Gen. 3:11 And he said, <u>Who told thee that thou wast naked?</u> Hast thou eaten of the tree, whereof I commanded thee that thou shouldest not eat?

They did not know how to fix their sin, so they used their wills to decide to cover it. It is interesting to note the question they did not answer in verse 11. They did not answer because they could not. It was an internal realization by a new fallen nature.

A verse that further confirms the blockage of man from being saved by his own understanding is found in Acts:

> Acts 28:27 For the heart of this people is waxed gross, and their ears are dull of hearing, and their eyes have they closed; <u>lest they should see with their eyes, and hear with their ears, and understand with their heart, and should be converted, and I should heal them.</u>

These impediments to understanding were not due to "bad luck" or inability on the part of unbelievers. The following verse confirms the Lord's prerogative to exercise control over the understanding of man. If man really has a free will, how is this verse not a blatant violation of that will?

> Deut. 29:4 <u>Yet the LORD hath not given you an heart to perceive, and eyes to see, and ears to hear, unto this day.</u>

A passage from 2 Corinthians tells us who the Lord uses as the agent for spiritual blindness.

> 2 Cor. 4:3 But <u>if our gospel be hid, it is hid to them that are lost</u>:

## BIBLICAL PERSPECTIVES ABOUT THE WILL OF MAN

> 2 Cor. 4:4 In whom <u>the god of this world hath blinded the minds of them which believe not</u>, lest the light of the glorious gospel of Christ, who is the image of God, should shine unto them.

Satan's blinding work afflicted all men in the Garden. Hence, it became God's foreordained work to enlighten the hearts of His elect. These verses confirm a purposeful working of God in the hearts of men. In Acts 28:27, Paul quoted the Holy Spirit as He spoke through Isaiah when he plainly stated that man's acknowledging of, and acceptance of, the Savior will never be solved by any action of "their own eyes," "their own ears," or "their own heart" that would obligate God to save them. Salvation can only be accomplished by His sovereign work that opens their eyes, ears, and hearts to understand and believe the gospel.

Does man perform the literal act of belief? Yes, but I would dare to equate it to the act of an infant drawing its first breath upon emerging from the womb. With his eyes, ears, and heart opened, a man now believes because he sees, hears, and understands. Man now exercises his enlightened will to believe the gospel because of what he has been divinely enabled to see, hear, and understand. Remember, as Luther, Edwards, and Zanchius taught, the will chooses want it wants. The Holy Spirit regenerates the hearts of God's elect at God's appointed time and in accordance with His sovereign will. Unbelievers and even many Christians, when recalling their life before they were saved, do not like to be told that they were in a spiritual captivity to Satan. Their attitude is that "my life is my life," and "I make my own decisions about believing or not believing." The shackles of their captivity may be invisible, but they are real, until the Holy Spirit breaks them. It is after salvation that we learn: I was a captive, this I know; the Holy Spirit opened my heart, this I know; Jesus chose me and saved me, this I know—for the Bible tells me so.

Scripture plainly records the Lord's active role in the understanding of men. He opened the understanding of the disciples

(Luke 24:45) and the heart of Lydia that she might believe (Acts 16:14). In Eph. 1:18, Paul asks for understanding to be enlightened and in Eph. 4:18 he talks about understanding being darkened. How can these understanding-altering works of the Lord be impartially performed among men with a free will? Does God open the understanding of every person who ever has lived or will live? Many free will defenders would answer, yes. From the free will perspective, for God to be fair to men in His judgment of them, He would have to open all hearts. They will point to verses like the following to support their answer.

> John 1:6 There was a man sent from God, whose name was John.

> John 1:7 The same came for a witness, to bear witness of the Light, that all men through him might believe.

This is a verse about the ministry of John the Baptist (verse 6). Was he able to witness to all men? The "all men" of this verse are all of those to whom he was able to witness to. The size of his audience was limited by time and space. Then Paul writes in Titus:

> Titus 2:11 For the grace of God that bringeth salvation hath appeared to all men,

Does this grace only start with the ministry of Jesus the man, or does it include the grace of God's creation itself, which should prompt the search by men for the creator? Does this "grace appearing" equate with the giving of understanding and the offer of saving faith? I submit that this "appearing" does not equal understanding by all men.

Some teachers believe the context of the expression "all men" in this verse means all sorts of men. The context of Titus, chapter 2 gives credence to this view. Preceding Titus 2:11, Paul gives instruction regarding "aged men," "aged women," "young women," "young men," "servants," and "masters". These categories of men (mankind) could reasonably comprise the "all men" that verse 11 refers to. But just because some form of grace has appeared to all men, it does not mean that all men have, or are given, comprehension of the offer of salvation. The Greek word for appearing is *epiphaino*, which means "to shine upon" or "become visible." Jesus and the gospel of salvation were lights that were not hidden by God under any bushel basket. The first light of grace is the knowledge of God that is manifest in all men.

> Rom. 1:19 Because <u>that which may be known of God is manifest in them</u> (**all men**); for God hath shewed it unto them.

Although these aforementioned grace lights have appeared to man, the rest of the story (as Paul Harvey would say), is that Satan is also hard at work blinding the eyes of all men from any gospel (salvation) offered to them until God opens their eyes, as previously cited in 2 Cor. 4:4. So Scripture tells us about both the appearing and the blinding work that happens to all men. But it must be understood that the "appearings" do not assure "understanding." The Jewish leadership of Jesus' day certainly did not understand and recognize Him as the prophesied Savior who was bringing salvation, in spite of Jesus plainly appearing to them. If any men should have seen and understood who Jesus was, it should have been the scribes and Pharisees. In Paul's day, the point was made that the salvation Christ brought was not just for the Jews only, but for the Gentiles as well. This was a shock for the Jewish leaders. They were taught by the Old Testament that the only way a Gentile could be saved was to become a proselyte to Judaism.

These "appearings" are steps that contribute to making all men responsible for seeking the God of creation. Creation itself is the first call of God to man. This call makes all men accountable for knowing that God exists. 1,500 years after the Garden of Eden, God resumed direct communication with man, starting with Abram. Then, as God continued to reveal Himself through the Law, the prophets, through Jesus' earthly ministry, and finally through the completed canon of Scripture, His call to men became increasingly explicit. The Scriptures reveal that man is a sinner in God's eyes, that he needs a savior, and that the salvation has been provided by the life, death, and resurrection of Jesus Christ. The Bible is one long progressive revelation of how God is accomplishing the redemption of His elect. God is able to get this explicit call to all who are His elect through teaching, the printed Word, or by direct dreams or visions. However, we also know from Scripture that many are called, but few are chosen.

Matt. 22:14 For many are called, but <u>few are chosen</u>.

1 Cor. 1:26 For ye see your calling, brethren, how that <u>not many</u> wise men after the flesh, not many mighty, not many noble, <u>are called</u>.

Notice that the word *all* does not appear in these verses. Furthermore, to those who are chosen, belief in Christ is granted by Christ. This, in turn, requires that understanding is given. If this granted belief is obtained by any other means than grace, then man is not saved by grace alone.

Phil. 1:29 For unto you **it is given** <u>in the behalf of Christ, not only to believe on him, but also to suffer for his sake;</u>

Eph. 1:18 The <u>eyes of your understanding being enlightened; that ye may know what is the hope of his calling</u>, and what the riches of the glory of his inheritance in the saints

The truths of the previous verses testify that a person's understanding must be opened in order to believe and that not everyone receives such an opening, because not all are chosen.

From the human perspective, the lack of a willingness to believe in salvation, apart from a working of God, does not exclude man from any responsibility to believe the gospel. I refer again to the scriptural truth that all men died in Adam because all men disbelieved God "in Adam". Adam understood that God was his creator. Adam understood the commands that God gave to him in Genesis 1 and 2. It was here that all men, likewise, existed in the same understanding. If it was not so, then all men would have to have understanding given to them at some other time, in order for all men to be held accountable for the sin of unbelief. That is why I believe that in Adam, all men were aware and able to obey. They had a truly "free will" with which to choose. They chose not to obey, and this is why, "in Adam, all die" (1 Cor. 15:22).

Since that time, while both God and man have a part in the belief decision, man alone cannot, and will not, initiate the salvation decision. This may sound like double-talk, but read what Luther asserted with regard to God's working in man:

> What I assert and maintain is this: where God works apart from the grace of His Spirit, He works all things in all men, even the ungodly; for He alone moves, makes to act and impels to the motion of His omnipotence, all those things which He alone created; they can neither avoid nor alter this movement, but necessarily follow and obey it, each thing according to the measure of its God-given power. Thus all things, even the ungodly, co-operate with God. And when God acts by the Spirit of his grace in those whom He has justified, that is, in His own kingdom, He moves and carries them along in like manner; and they, being a new creation, follow and co-operate with Him, or rather, as Paul says are made to act by Him. (Rom. 8:14)[37]

Rom. 8:14 For as many as are <u>led by the Spirit of God</u>, they are the sons of God.

---

[37] Luther, 267-268.

Stop and consider the irony and the mystery of this "way" of God. He allowed man to lose his eternal life by an act of his own created free will, but, since then, will not allow man to reclaim what he lost by any independent act of his own, now fallen, will. It may seem incomprehensible to men, but we must yield to this truth:

> Rom. 11:33 O the depth of the riches both of the wisdom and knowledge of God! how unsearchable are his judgments, and his ways past finding out!

The term *free will* is true only in the context that every man is free to choose what he wants <u>within the limits of his nature</u>. The adjective free, as used in the Arminian context, is equivalent to the word *able*. I believe Scripture confirms that the will of all of Adam's posterity is no longer free in regard to being able to believe the gospel for salvation, apart from God's sovereign, regenerating work. I believe that this is the deeper implication of John 8:36.

> John 8:36 <u>If the Son therefore shall make you free, ye shall be free indeed</u>.

Mankind likes to think he has a free will, but only Jesus can make anyone "free indeed"; free from their bondage in sin.

CHAPTER 8

# Assorted Thoughts and Some Views of Others on Free Will

**Free Will—Put in Perspective**

IF THE AVERAGE PERSON is asked the point-blank question, "Does man have a free will?" a majority will reflexively answer, "Yes." Their answer is no surprise. Why? Their lives are a succession of choices made for the ultimate reason of doing what they want. One could protest that they have done many things contrary to what they wanted. I think it is a safe presumption that a majority of working people, who are not yet retired, would testify that there are numerous mornings when they don't want to get out of bed and go to work. But they do so because the desire to provide for their families and to not lose their job is a stronger "want" than is the "want" of staying in bed. So, ultimately, getting out of bed and going to work is also an example of doing what they want most.

It is an undeniable fact, as Edwards writes, that men do what they will to do in all their choices. If the question is not investigated any deeper, then at the superficial level, it seems that men do have a free will. It is especially true of unsaved men, because they have no clue of the depth of their bondage to their fallen nature. They never see how this nature drives their choices continually. Sadly, many Christians also accept free will as a fact of their life. To them, the Bible is relegated to being God's lengthy sales pitch for salvation that awaits their free will choice of acceptance or rejection. Just one more decision they must make.

**Words Are Important**

If words have meaning and God deems to use certain words in certain places in Scripture to describe His works, then their true meaning is all-important. The Bible teacher I referenced at the beginning of this book, Les Feldick, whose lessons we use in our home Bible study group, is always quick to point out what he calls "time words" as he exposits Scripture: such words as *then, when, until, now,* and *but now,* for example. He reminds his audiences that they are signposts that alert the reader that something new or different is about to be revealed. He stresses the importance of understanding verses that surround such time words in their proper context. His points about time words are well made.

In the context of time words, I ask you to consider the following special category of time words that define the sovereign acts of God. They deserve equal attention to the time words just mentioned. Three words in particular I will refer to are "before the beginning" time words: *predestinated, foreordained,* and *foreknow* indicate, by the prefixes "pre" and "fore," that these verbs have a time context that always means before the beginning of time. Their appearances in the Bible are:

predestinated: 2 times (Eph. 1: 5, 11)
foreordained: 1 time (1 Pet. 1:20)
foreknow 1 time (Rom. 8:29)

Two other words that are often, but not always, connected to actions of God done before time began are *ordained* and *determined*. They appear in both contexts, either as an action by men "in time" or as an action by God "before time." Their usages are:

ordained: 10 times +/- (by my count, when referring to direct acts of God)
determined: 6 times (by my count, when referring to direct acts of God)

Because God is eternal, there are several verses that tell us of actions He took before time began, using many of the words above. The phrase "from the beginning" is used 39 times in scripture, at least 25 times referring to before creation. When words are used to describe acts of God, the outcomes of these acts are, or will be, inevitable. These word usages are given to us for the express purpose of proclaiming God's eternal being and His sovereignty. These words also carry a force of meaning that divorces the particular act it modifies from any dependence upon man or his circumstances. The existence of the large number of Christians, who deny the truth of election to salvation, reveals the fact that man chaffs under the proposition that God would or could do such a thing as choose some to salvation and pass by others, or that He would override their "free will".

It is an expository stretch made by theologians who detach the words *predestinated*, *foreordained*, *foreknow*, *ordained*, and *determined*, from any connection to the act of God's sovereign choosing of certain persons to salvation. Here is a verse that makes this choosing work of God to salvation virtually impossible to deny:

2 Thess. 2:13 But we are bound to give thanks always to God for you, brethren beloved of the Lord, because <u>God hath from the beginning chosen you to salvation through sanctification of the Spirit and belief of the truth</u>:

This verse declares that God chose specific persons, "you," for a specific end, "salvation," by specific means "through sanctification of the Spirit and belief of the truth."

However, if man's free will is the trigger that moved God to choose who will be saved, then it unavoidably subordinates the power and force of the phrase "from the beginning" to man's free will. As previously stated, free will doctrine diminishes any glory given to God for His "pre-time" choices regarding salvation because it proposes that such choices are contingent upon man's "within time" decision to believe.

Accordingly, the "choosing to salvation" of 2 Thess. 2:13 would become an obligation of God because of the misconception that it must be man's free will choice to accept salvation. This is the logic path that free will doctrine creates. Every believer should be taught from Scripture if it is God's will or man's will that is the first cause of salvation. Sadly, most Christians leave the answer to their teachers and pastors, and most of these don't produce an answer that comes from the whole counsel of God.

**The Paradox of Free Will**

Earlier I noted the controversial adjectives on the Calvinist side of the argument. On the Arminian side we find that it has just one controversial adjective that defines their theology—the adjective "free." Dr. Vance acknowledges the importance of this word as a definer of man's will. He states: The debate over man's will hinges upon the meaning of the word *free*.[38]

---

38 Vance, 202.

The adjective *"free"* has had multiple interpretations attached to it by both sides of the debate. It has been my experience that those who adhere to the free will viewpoint struggle with providing a clear definition of this word. But, whatever else it may mean, on the Arminian (free will) side, as it relates to the salvation decision, it must imply a freedom from any Divine compulsion, intrusion, or influence that would cause a person to believe. The concepts of a "free" will choice to believe and God's sovereign choice of election of some to salvation are logically contradictory. But this has not stopped some Christians from trying to incorporate both into their belief system.

**Two Attempts at Compromise**

**1. Dr. Norman Geisler**

Dr. Norman Geisler provides an example of a compromised solution. The title of one of his books is *Chosen, But Free*. By this very title, there is a suggestion that these two concepts coexist in some state of equality. Read carefully the words of the following paragraph as Dr. Geisler tries to justify both concepts and fold them into a workable theology:

> Why, then, does one person go to heaven and another not? Because God willed that all who receive His grace will be saved and that all who reject it will be lost. And since God knew infallibly just who this would be, both the elect and the non-elect were determined from all eternity. And this determination was not based on anything in man, including their free choice. Rather, it was determined on God's choice to save all who would accept His unconditional grace.[39]

If you can read and swallow this conclusion of Dr. Geisler and think that it resolves the contradiction, you are not paying

---

39 Norman Geisler, *Chosen, But Free*. (Minneapolis: Bethany House Publishers, 2010), 185–186.

very close attention to what he wrote. He offers a fine example of circular logic that gives no cause and effect relationship between God's sovereignty and man's free will. Let's analyze these five sentences to track their logic, if possible. My commentary is inserted in italics:

Why, then, does one person go to heaven and another not? (*This is the essential question.*)

Because God willed that all who receive His grace will be saved and that all who reject it will be lost. (*A biblical truth, but it gives no indication of why or how anyone "receives." Is it by mental deduction or by merely a lucky choice?*)

And since God knew infallibly just who this would be, both the elect and the non-elect were determined from all eternity. (*This is slightly misleading. God's knowing was not the determiner of the elect and the non-elect. His will and eternal purpose are the determiners. If God's foreknowledge was the cause of election and non-election, imagine your arrival in heaven and coming face-to-face with Jesus. You would say to Him, "Thank You for choosing me," and Jesus would then respond, "Thanks for believing. I knew you would."*)

And this determination was not based on anything in man, including their free choice. (*The first part of this sentence is true. The second part suggests that there is such a thing as free will. But, while it denies that free will had any part in the determination, Dr.Geisler offers no clue as to how free will fits into the salvation equation.*)

Rather, it was determined on God's choice to save all, who would accept His unconditional grace. (*Dr.Geisler concludes with a cause and effect statement. If you will read the preceding sentence, you will notice that Dr.Geisler has flatly contradicted it in his last sentence. In the preceding sentence, he openly dismissed any causative role of man's free will. Then he concludes by saying God's saving was determined upon all whom, "would accept His unconditional grace." How and why did they "accept"? That is the question Dr.Geisler does not answer.)*

Although this last statement is a cause and effect statement, it is a hypothetical statement about any of the "all who would accept," similar to the biblical counterpart, John 3:16, which refers to the hypothetical "whosoever believeth." But Dr, Geisler neglects to explain the reason for why anyone accepts the unconditional grace. He states a true fact that both sovereignty and free will exist in Scripture. He tries to establish a neutral position on the matter by accusing both Calvinists and Arminians of distorting the truths of sovereignty and free will respectively. He writes:

> Sovereignty and free will. Is it one or the other, or is it both one and the other? The Bible says both.[40]

The sovereignty of God is revealed without question in scripture. The actual term "free will" does not appear anywhere in the Bible. Although men's decision-making ability is on display throughout the Bible, I do not see how it can ever unquestionably be labeled as being truly free, apart from of Adam and Eve. The freedom of their wills was evidenced from their choice to disobey while they were yet "good" creations of God. Also, there is no clear biblical indication that men's will remained free to overrule their fallen nature with regard to salvation. To the contrary, it has been previously documented by many verses that testify to man's captive status and his enmity with God. What Dr. Geisler neglects to define is his assertion of both how and when these biblical facts of sovereignty and free will, enter into man's salvation decision. Dr. Geisler's circular attempt to accommodate both God's sovereign choosing and man's free will choosing, in regard to election or non-election, fails.

---

40 Ibid, 37.

The point was made in the introduction of this book that the issue of how salvation is initiated has only two sides—God's sovereignty or man's free will. It was also postulated that there is no middle theological ground between these sides. All Christians stand on one side or the other. Dr. Geisler strains to find a middle ground, but his logic collapses. He was not wrong in saying that there is such a reality as free will in the Bible. He just fails to recognize its demise, which occurred when Adam sinned. Although Dr. Geisler dismissed free will from any part of the salvation of man, by his statement that God's choice was the result of man's "acceptance of His unconditional grace," Dr. Geisler pitches his tent in the Arminian camp. The Arminians, however, might expel him outside their camp because of his theory that denies free will any part in the salvation decision. Try as he might, Dr. Geisler has nowhere else to go on this debate.

## 2. Dr. C. Gordon Olsen

Another attempt at a compromise theology comes from Dr. C. Gordon Olson, who authored a 538-page work titled, *Beyond Calvinism and Arminianism: An Inductive Mediate Theology of Salvation*.[41] Here is another book title proposing that an alternate biblical position exists between Calvinism and Arminianism. A nutshell synopsis of Dr. Olson's work is found on the back cover of his book. It reads:

> Calvinists and Arminians are at opposite poles on the question of how God applies the merits of Christ's saving death to sinners. Few recognize any mediate view between opposite views, with mainstream Evangelicals who are not fully committed to either system. Olson seeks a resolution to this

---

41 C. Gordon Olson, *Beyond Calvinism & Arminianism*. (Cedar Knolls, NJ: Global Gospel Publishers, 2002.

## ASSORTED THOUGHTS AND SOME VIEWS OF OTHERS ON FREE WILL

conflict by an inductive rather than a deductive approach to Scripture."[42]

I cite this book because of its deceptive title, subtitle, and premise. Based on his "mediate" position premise, I think Dr. Olsen's book should have been titled, *Between Calvinism and Arminianism*. I label the premise behind his book title and subtitle as being deceptive because Dr. Olson's book is, in reality, just another Arminian salvo aimed at the doctrine of God's sovereign in salvation (commonly labeled Calvinism or determinism). Lest you think I am unjustly defensive in this assessment of Dr. Olson's book by calling it an Arminian attack, I offer 3 selections from a complimentary review of his book as found on the website faithalone.org. This review was written by another prominent Arminian theologian.

> One of the strengths of the Calvinistic system is the monopoly on books about Calvinism that it has long held. Until recently, most books written in opposition to Calvinism were either small pamphlets inherently limited in their effectiveness or works from the equally objectionable Arminian point of view. The tide has gradually shifted over the past twenty years, and especially during the last five or six. There is Norman Geisler's Chosen But Free (1999, 2001 revised edition), Dave Hunt's What Love is This? (2002), Robert Picirilli's Grace, Faith, Free Will (2002), and my own contribution, The Other Side of Calvinism (1999 revised edition). The new book by C. Gordon Olson, Beyond Calvinism and Arminianism: An Inductive Mediate Theology of Salvation, is a welcome addition to the growing number of books that offer an alternative to Calvinism....
>
> ... True to its title, Beyond Calvinism and Arminianism focuses on the theology of salvation, but within the general framework of the Calvinist/Arminian debate. This allows Olsen to broaden his approach while focusing on what he considers

---

42 Ibid, back cover synopsis.

to be the problems with Calvinism, of which he finds a great deal....

... This book is a valuable addition to the growing body of literature on the subject of Calvinism."[43]

This reviewer is under no illusion about what Dr. Olson's target was. The reviewer was none other than Dr. Laurence M. Vance, whose book was a major focus of my critique of Arminianism.

The reason I make mention of Dr. Olson's book and Dr. Vance's review of it is to enforce my assertion of the clear distinction that divides these two "poles." To put a finer point (or should I say, "a sharper edge") on the divide in this ancient debate, we find on one side a clear, but narrow position that rests solidly upon the view that salvation is the sole, 100 percent work of God. In stark contrast, on the other side of the divide, there are 99 other possible positions that must incorporate some degree of human contribution to the act of salvation. To be theologically honest, any position that assigns any percentage of human involvement in salvation to man must be properly labeled as Arminian. Whether one's theological formula presents salvation as the result of 99 percent man's effort and 1 percent God's work or 99 percent God's work and a 1 percent contribution by man, or by any percentage division that rests between these two extremes, it is still Arminianism. It is a rose by any other name, regardless of whatever label is given to it—like, for instance, the label "mediate."

It should be logically clear that there is no third position. Any position that asserts one hundred percent Arminianism, which would mean salvation by total human effort and zero effort by

---

[43] Lawrence M. Vance, review of *Beyond Calvinism & Arminianism: An Inductive Mediate Theology of Salvation* by C. Gordon Olsen, *Journal of the Grace Evangelical Society*, Book Reviews, http://faithalone.org/journal/bookreviews/olson.html.

an uninvolved God, does not exist. The logical implication of such a view would collapse with contradictions. It would imply that man is saved by 100 percent of his own effort by a God who had nothing to do with it—including the atoning work of Jesus Christ. This is ludicrous. Thus, there is a clear theological divide. Any compromise formula offered is still some variety of Arminianism. So the question remains: Is salvation by some combination work of God and man, or is it God's sovereign work alone, accomplished according to His will and foreordained purpose alone?

## An Uncompromised Conclusion

### Dr. Hobart E. Freeman

Theologian Dr. Hobart E. Freeman, in his book titled *Divine Sovereignty, Human Freedom*, comes to a more solid and unassailable conclusion about the paradox of these two biblical realities. He writes:

> The truth of man's freedom, while it is a reality, can never be understood, if it is divorced from two other Biblical concepts. One is the fact of man's own sinful nature which severely circumscribes the direction in which his freedom will be operative. "Man is free to do as he wishes" is an oft-heard refrain. However, in the moral and spiritual realm, history and the Scriptures give ample evidence that this freedom is universally operative in one direction only and on one plane only. Jeremiah confirms this when he charges that the nation of Israel lives in a state of "perpetual backsliding." (Jeremiah 8:5).

(Jer. 8:5 Why then is this people of Jerusalem slidden back by a perpetual backsliding? they hold fast deceit, they refuse to return.)

Isaiah likewise traces Israel's wickedness from her very beginning:

> Isa. 48:8 Yea, thou heardest not; yea, thou knewest not; yea, from that time that thine ear was not opened: for I knew that thou wouldest deal very treacherously, and wast called a transgressor from the womb.

The people were so submerged in their sinfulness and willful disobedience that they could not even hear the Lord when He called:

> Isa. 65:2 I have spread out my hands all the day unto a rebellious people, which walketh in a way that was not good, after their own thoughts;

Man may be free, but it is not in him by nature to direct his steps Godward, contends Jeremiah:

> Jer. 10:23 O Lord, I know that <u>the way of man is not in himself: it is not in man that walketh to direct his steps</u>.

> Jer. 10:24 O Lord, correct me, but with judgment; not in thine anger, lest thou bring me to nothing.

> Jer. 13:23 Can the Ethiopian change his skin, or the leopard his spots? <u>then may ye also do good, that are accustomed to do evil</u>.

Men may argue and philosophize over the question of the absolute free-will of man, his power of choice, and the uniqueness of his independence; but the prophets insist that apart from grace, which alone can replace the heart of stone with a spiritual heart and redirect the will, sinful man will invariably choose what his unregenerate heart desires most—sin and self. Without this new heart, then men can no more choose good who are accustomed to practicing evil, than the Ethiopian can make himself white or the leopard remove his spots. Paradoxically enough, man's freedom, apart from grace, becomes a fearful specter, an enemy to the soul, a power to enslave him to bondage and ultimate destruction. This, as has been shown, does not mean that he lacks the capacity to will the good; but rather, he lacks the kind of heart that desires the good. What man believes to be his greatest power and glory, his freedom of will, is in reality his greatest weakness apart from grace. The most dreadful nemesis of man is his freedom to choose as he pleases.[44]

I concur with Dr. Freeman. He has the correct biblical perspective regarding man's will as a will that is free to do "what a man wants." He sees free will for what it is and what it did to man. Man's will is properly identified as the "dreadful nemesis" of man's fallen and helpless condition, while God's salvation by His elective grace is the only true solution to overcoming man's fall into the condemnation of sin. Sovereign election to salvation defeats the failure caused by man's free will. Dr. Freeman's conclusions are in stark contrast to Dr. Geisler and Dr. Olsen, who valiantly try, but fail, to spin these two truths into a workable theology on an equal footing.

---

44 Hobart Freeman, *Divine Sovereignty, Human Freedom.* (Warsaw, IN: Faith Ministries & Publications, 1990), 185–187.

CHAPTER 9

# Election Why?, Who?, What? and Man's Hatred of It

THE WORDS SUCH AS *predestinated*, *foreordained*, and *foreknow*, that were discussed in the previous chapter, provide support for the controversial doctrine of election. These words enforce the fact that all salvations are by God's will and not man's will. The doctrine of election is quite possibly the greatest stumbling block in all of theology. It sends much of Christianity into a theological frenzy. This doctrine prompts the following questions of why, who, what, and how. It stokes Christian passions, and a great deal of that passion is hatred.

**Why Does God Save by Election?**

Since God is omniscient and cannot learn anything new, it was no surprise to Him that men would not and could not meet

His standards of obedience, apart from Him. It was no surprise to Him when Adam and Eve sinned. A thinking person should ask at this point, "Then why did God do it this way?" When men question God's elective prerogative, they are rebuked in Romans:

> Rom. 9:20 Nay but, O man, who art thou that repliest against God? Shall the thing formed say to him that formed it, <u>Why hast thou made me thus?</u>

I suggest that the answer to the question is to prove two things to men. The first is their need for a Savior. When Jesus made the following statement in chapter 15 of John's gospel that defined man's helplessness, I suspect He was not just referring to fruit bearing.

> John 15:5 I am the vine, ye are the branches: He that abideth in me, and I in him, the same bringeth forth much fruit: for <u>without me ye can do nothing.</u>

Disconcerting as it may be to Arminians, "nothing" means nothing. This "nothing" includes saving belief. If man's helplessness does not include his act of belief in the gospel, then why are we told these facts about lost men and what God does to bring them to belief? Consider the following verses and the points of interpretation below each verse:

> Eph. 2:1 And <u>you hath he quickened, who were dead in trespasses and sins.</u>

(Men were "dead," not just ill. The dead can't decide not to be dead.)

> Eph. 2:3 Among whom also <u>we all</u> had our conversation in times past in the lusts of our flesh, fulfilling the desires of the flesh and of the mind; and <u>were by nature the children of wrath</u>, even as others.

(Men's nature was as "children of wrath." Men cannot decide to change their nature any more than a leopard can decide to change his spots.)

> Eph. 2:8 For by grace are ye <u>saved through faith; and that not of yourselves: it is the gift of God</u>.

(The faith, by which we believe, was itself a gift of God. Spiritually dead men cannot generate their own faith. This point will be developed and explained in Chapter 10.)

> 2 Tim. 1:9 Who <u>hath saved us, and called us</u> with an holy calling, not according to our works, but <u>according to his own purpose and grace</u>, which was <u>given us in Christ Jesus before the world began</u>,

(This verse alone answers the question of why God saved us in the manner He did.)

The second reason for God's elective method of salvation is to reveal the glory of His grace. Listen to what it says in Ephesians 1 that God did for us to reveal the glory of His grace:

> Eph. 1:3 Blessed be the God and Father of our Lord Jesus Christ, who <u>hath blessed us with all spiritual blessings in heavenly places in Christ</u>:

> Eph. 1:4 According as he <u>hath chosen us in him before the foundation of the world</u>, that we should be holy and without blame before him in love:

> Eph. 1:5 Having <u>predestinated us unto the adoption of children by Jesus Christ to himself</u>, according <u>to the good pleasure of his will</u>,

## What did God do?

In verse 3, He <u>blessed us</u> with all spiritual blessings in heavenly places in Christ.

In verse 4, He hath <u>chosen us</u> in him before the foundation of the world, that we should be holy and without blame before him in love.

In verse 5, He <u>predestinated us</u> unto the adoption of children by Jesus Christ to himself.

**To what purpose?**

> Eph. 1:6 <u>To the praise of the glory of his grace</u>, wherein he hath made us accepted in the beloved.

And again,

> 2 Tim.1:9 Who hath saved us, and called us with an holy calling, not according to our works, but <u>according to his own purpose and grace, which was given us in Christ Jesus before the world began,</u>

God has told us why He saved men by His election, yet many Christians hate the idea that God predestinates anyone.

Read again the truths of Ephesians 1:

> Eph. 1:3 Blessed be the God and Father of our Lord Jesus Christ, who <u>hath blessed us with all spiritual blessings in heavenly places in Christ:</u>

> Eph. 1:4 According as he <u>hath chosen us in him before the foundation of the world</u>, that we should be holy and without blame before him in love:

> Eph. 1:5 Having <u>predestinated us unto the adoption of children by Jesus Christ to himself</u>, according to the good pleasure of his will,

# ELECTION WHY?, WHO?, WHAT? AND MAN'S HATRED OF IT

To demonstrate that many Christians detest the thought of election to salvation, I have often heard many preachers and teachers try to divert God's choosing activity in verse 4 and His predestinating activity in verse 5 away from the topic of salvation. They insist that His "choosing" was to our being "holy and without blame," not salvation. Likewise, they teach that we were predestined "unto the adoption of children" rather than to salvation. They gladly point out that the word "salvation" is missing from these verses.

Rather than demonstrate their scholarship and expositional prowess, their attempts to separate salvation from
1. being "blessed with all spiritual blessings,"
2. being "chosen from before the foundation of the world, that we should be holy and without blame before Him, in love," and
3. being "predestinated unto the adoption of children by Jesus Christ to himself,"

only serve to show how desperate they are to preserve the place of man's free will in his salvation. Trying to separate salvation from any equivalency to the three blessings of verses 3, 4, and 5 is like trying to remove sugar from your iced tea. These blessings are part and parcel of being saved. The word salvation could be added in parentheses behind any of these blessings without distorting the meaning of the verses. These verses are God's revealing to us the place these three blessings have in His eternal plan for His elect. Opponents may insist that it is not illogical to claim that these blessings of being chosen and predestinated, were contingent upon a man's saving act of belief. However, if such was the case, then these blessings become a sovereign reward for man's free will work of belief, rather than part of a Divine gift that is part and parcel of salvation.

The natural inclination of even many Christians to reject the thought that election is to salvation is evidence that the old nature is still operative, (men retaining their identities as their own "god" or as being the "god" of their own life) is still operative. Paul lamented in Romans 7 that this old nature is still alive and active. If the distorters of the truth about election would look at the multiple uses of the term "elect" (16) and "election" (6) in the New Testament, it must be evident that it has a special meaning for anyone to be so designated by God. Election means more than just being chosen to be "holy and without blame before Him, in love" or just predestined to "the adoption of children by Jesus Christ to himself." If this was the extent of what it means to be "God's elect," then it cannot be denied that a believer retains the boast that this designation could not have happened without his consent to it. Why? It is due to the myth that free will is the cause of election.

**Who Are God's Elect? Two Types of Men**

So is everyone made free indeed as John 8:36 tells us? God was pretty specific in Romans chapter 9 when a clear delineation was made between the two types of vessels that would populate His creation. With "vessels" being a metaphor for types of men, we are told that God made vessels of mercy "which he afore prepared (predestined) for glory":

> Rom. 9:23 And that he might make known the riches of his glory on <u>the vessels of mercy, which he had afore prepared unto glory,</u>

Lest we think that all men are potentially "vessels of mercy," we are also told of the necessary, yet negative, side of this truth that cannot be denied. By default, those not "afore prepared unto glory" must be those "vessels fitted for destruction." If the vessels of mercy were so prepared "afore," then the "vessels fitted for destruction" were likewise so prepared "afore" for their destiny.

> Rom. 9:22 What if God, willing to shew his wrath, and to make his power known, endured with much longsuffering <u>the vessels of wrath fitted to destruction</u>.

The most misunderstood truth about the "enduring " of the "vessels fitted for destruction" is what caused their position. Their own choice to sin was what made them fit for destruction. Their being "fitted for destruction" was by God's act of not electing (choosing) to save them from their sin, but it was not God's causing them to sin. Re-read these sentences again carefully. These verses in Romans 9 are distinct examples of God telling us about one of His secrets but not telling us any of the particulars—like who is which vessel. He tells us that there will be a specific day that Christ will return to earth, but the day and the hour remain His secret. Likewise is the secret of His knowledge of who He has chosen before the foundation of time for salvation and who is passed over in His sovereign prerogative. We don't know everything God knows. These are two examples of such secrets that He tells us of, but that remain unrevealed. Remember,"For my thoughts are not your thoughts, neither are your ways my ways, saith the Lord," (Isa. 55:8) and "The secret things belong unto the Lord our God: but those things which are revealed belong unto us and to our children forever, that we may do all the words of this law" (Deut. 29:29) .

This is the essential truth about the topic of predestination that many Christians do not, or will not, grasp. The point is that God, to magnify the extent of His grace and His sovereignty, has told us of the fact of His predestinating work, but He tells no one about who are the chosen and who are not, so that "the purpose of election might stand." We are told of the "fact" of predestination, but not the "who" of predestination. Many Christians are unwilling to let God be God and believe Him in this matter. Does their denial of predestination negate their salvation? No. Does it detract from the glory they can give God? Yes, because of their belief that some degree of their salvation relies upon an act of their free will.

## What Is the Purpose of Election?

> Rom. 9:11 (For the children being not yet born, neither having done any good or evil, <u>that the purpose of God according to election might stand</u>, not of works, but of him that calleth.)

Just what could that purpose of God's election, be? It is an election that He tells the fact of, but not the details. Two purposes come to my mind. First, the Bible is clear that God determined that those who are saved by faith in the gospel are also to be the conveyors of the same gospel message by which He will save others. It is one of the common charges leveled by Arminians against the doctrine of election to salvation that, if it were true, then the work of evangelism is pointless. The reason offered for such pointlessness is that because God knows whom He is going to save, any evangelizing efforts of man are unnecessary. But Arminians neglect the truth that God will not allow man to have, or to presume to have, any knowledge about who are His chosen vessels but, as yet, are not saved. Therefore, God wants those who have been saved to view all unsaved men as possible vessels prepared for glory. The obedience of believers to evangelize non-believers brings glory to God because it is work done by their faith, and because they can't know, or presume to know, who will be saved. God will have mercy in salvation upon whom He will. Belief in the truth of election is an act of faith. Evangelism is an act of faith. Believer's acts of faith are the only way to please God.

> Heb. 11:6 But without faith it is impossible to please him.

In this way, God also gets glory by how He prevails over Satan. Consider the beauty of this "way" of God. In the Garden, Satan was allowed to steal the crown jewel of God's creation, man, who was made in the image of God. God, in turn, redeems this stolen jewel by power of His Word, through the very agency of man, by using redeemed men to convey salvation to other lost men. It is a saving process that Satan is powerless to stop, even though he never stops trying.

The second purpose in God's election is to assert His sovereignty over salvation. It preserves and demonstrates His glory for 100 percent grace in salvation. Like it or not, God sovereignly enables each of His elect (who, before their salvation, are unaware of their own election) to willfully respond in their belief of the gospel. Without God's sovereign enablement, called the "washing of regeneration performed by the Holy Ghost" in Titus 3:5, no one could be saved.

One of the most frequent heresies put forward by free will advocates is the one that states God elected (before time) those who (by their free will) will choose (in time) to believe the gospel. By this heresy the doctrine of election is trivialized, because it asserts that anyone's election to salvation by God (Eph. 1:13), was contingent upon a man's choosing to believe God. Maybe the word "insults" is more accurate. By using the free will of man in this context, it means that God elects people because of an obligation to do so.

Events that God allowed to occur in direct opposition to Him, such as Satan's rebellion and Adam's disobedience, were all overcome by His sovereign decrees and by His grace alone. But in the context of salvation, according to free will (Arminian) doctrine, the sanctity of man's free will decision is, in theory, allowed to continue. By their doctrine, man's choice becomes the first cause, (*primam causam*, as Luther or Zanchius would have put it) of his own salvation. God's choice, therefore, is but a reaction to man's choice. As previously stated, this restriction of God's choice insults His sovereignty. The purpose of election must stand and it must be sovereign.

> Rom. 9:8 That is, They which are the children of the flesh, these are not the children of God: but the <u>children of the promise are counted for the seed</u>.

> Rom. 9:11 For the children being not yet born, neither having done any good or evil, <u>that the purpose of God according to election might stand, not of works, but of him that calleth</u>.

(If I was allowed to put a finer point on this verse, I would add after the phrase "not of works" the phrase "and not of man's free choice." Nevertheless, I will prove in the next chapter that "free will" saving faith is really a work. Thus my editing of Rom. 9:11 is not needed.)

God reigns over everything, including salvation.

> 1 Chron. 16:31 Let the heavens be glad, and let the earth rejoice: and let men say among the nations, <u>the LORD reigneth</u>.

> Dan. 4:35 And all the inhabitants of the earth are reputed as nothing: and <u>he doeth according to his will in the army of heaven, and among the inhabitants of the earth</u>: and none can stay his hand, or say unto him, What doest thou?

> Ps. 3:8 <u>Salvation belongeth unto the LORD</u>: thy blessing is upon thy people. Selah.

I suggest that free will doctrine rebels against the thrust of these verses by its contention that no man can be saved until he decides to be saved, God's sovereignty notwithstanding. Arminian theology's stand on free will says, in effect, that man's free will can stay God's hand with regard to salvation. This explains their total refusal of the "I" of the Calvinism's TULIP—Irresistible Grace.

Scripture tells us that God, who is not bound by time in His knowledge or actions, overcame the fallen wills of His elect by

His choosing to save them before the foundation of the world. Therefore, the salvation of His elect was never contingent upon their act of will. Rather, the exercise of their will in belief of the gospel was contingent upon the work of the Holy Spirit upon their hearts, as God's foreordained elect. This is clearly stated in John's gospel regarding those who receive and believe on His name.

> John 1:12 But <u>as many as received him,</u>(believed in Christ) to them gave he power to become the sons of God, even to them <u>that believe on his name</u>:

> John 1:13 <u>Which were born, not of blood, nor of the will of the flesh, nor of the will of man, but of God</u>.

and

> John 6:44 <u>No man can come to me, except the Father which hath sent me draw him</u>: and I will raise him up at the last day.

> John 6:65 And he said, Therefore said I unto you, that <u>no man can come unto me, except it were given unto him of my Father.</u>

This drawing must be the work of the Holy Spirit as we are shown in Romans 8 and Titus 3.

> Rom. 8:14 <u>For as many as are led by the Spirit of God, they are the sons of God</u>.

> Gal. 5:18 But if ye <u>be led of the Spirit</u>, ye are not under the law.

Titus 3:5 Not by works of righteousness which we have done, but according to his mercy <u>he saved us, by the washing of regeneration, and renewing of the Holy Ghost</u>.

The doctrine of free will is incompatible with the doctrine of God's sovereign election to salvation as these verses confirm. Any effort to create an interdependency between these two doctrines must logically subordinate God's act of election to man's free will.

**Men's Hatred of Election**

It is a sad but true fact, that men, even many believers, tend to hate the doctrine of election. An eighteenth-century hymn writer, Joseph Hart, penned the chorus below that expresses man's hatred of the doctrine of election; a hatred that exists among many Christians today.

> Why so offensive in their eyes
> Does God's election seem?
> Because they think themselves so wise
> That they have chosen Him. . . .
> "Election!" 'tis a word divine;
> For, Lord, I plainly see,
> Had not, Thy choice preceded mine,
> I ne'er had chosen Thee.[45]

If I could add a stanza with Mr. Hart's permission, I would append the following to his lyrics:

> Why so proud in the hearts of men,
> Does the power of their will make God depend?
> His blessing of election is all for naught
> If upon man's choice, saving grace is wrought.

---

[45] Joseph Hart, "What Makes Mistaken Men Afraid?" in "Elected Unto Salvation: A Hated Doctrine of Churchianity," by Daniel Parks, http://www.gracegospel.org.uk/election_to_salvation.htm.

## Election and the Biblical Sequence of Salvation

Free will doctrine must make a direct assault on the doctrine of election. God's grace in His act of election of some individuals to salvation is at the head of a sequence of events that culminate in the elect individual's act of belief in the gospel. The mystery of salvation is found in the fact that the elect individual not only does not know of his election prior to his belief, but he or she is also unaware of the occurrence of any of four prior steps of this sequence, listed below, prior to the very moment of their belief in the only gospel for today (1 Cor. 15:3-4).

There are five elements that lead to and culminate in salvation. The biblical and, I believe, chronological sequence of salvation from God's perspective reads:

**Election to Salvation before Time by God's will -> A Hearing of the Word of God -> The Heart Opened to Understanding -> The Gift of Faith Given -> Belief of the Gospel**

(The -> symbol above could be supplanted with the words "leads to". . ." showing the cause and effect chain of the salvation sequence.)

If this order of the salvation sequence is at all confusing to the reader, let me present the same sequence, in reverse, from the saved individual's viewpoint. I will display it in a Q and A format. The questions below are ones that every believer should ask. I will start at the occasion of a believer's moment of belief:

*Start*: At some point in their life, a person is moved to confess with their mouth and believe in their heart (Rom. 10:9) that Jesus Christ is the Son of God who was crucified according to the Scriptures, was buried, and rose again on the third day according to the Scriptures (1 Cor. 15:3-4). This belief secures their salvation.

*Question 1.* Why did the person believe, or what caused them to move from their natural state of unbelief to the spiritual state of belief?

*Answer 1.* They received from God the gift of faith by grace (Eph. 2:8–9).

*Question 2.* What led to the person being given the gift of faith?

*Answer 2.* Their heart was opened by God to understand a word of God that they just heard. Like Lydia (Acts 16:14) and like the disciples (Luke 24:45), they were enabled to understand what they needed and why. Luke 24:45 "Then opened he their understanding, that they might understand the scriptures,"

*Question 3.* What was it the person heard that their heart was opened to?

*Answer 3.* They heard the Word of God that is the mandated transmitter of faith. (Rom. 10:17). They heard it by either sight, sound or by a God-given vision or dream.

*Question 4.* The combined occurence of the events of answers 1, 2, and 3 are labeled as "effectual hearing." How is it determines who gets the "effectual hearing" sequence that leads to saving faith?

*Answer 4.* Before the foundation of the world, God chose (elected) all whom He would save (Eph. 1:4–5), according to "the good pleasure of His will"—not the individual's will. God is the determiner of the recipients of the "effectual hearing" sequence that produces salvation.

*Question 5.* Why then, did God choose (elect) me?

*Answer 5.* There is only one answer to this question. There is no reason within any person that caused God's election of a person, including their willful choice to believe. The willful choice by anyone to believe was the result of God's work of grace in answers 1,2, and 3. It was totally done by God's pre-creation pleasure of His good will to do so. Thus, the short answer and only answer to this "why" question is, "by His grace alone!"

These five truths, in whichever order you view them, form the prerequisite, God-ordained, biblically supported sequence that produces salvation. The election, by God of some individuals to salvation, happened before the foundation of time. It is the spark that ignites the salvation sequence. The sequence and its culmination in belief happens in God's "due time" to each elect individual. If the first step is God's predestinating election is a certainty, then all of the intervening steps and the end result of saving faith in the elect are also certainties. God will save all of those whom He has chosen by His election. These five truths produce the only bridge of saving faith across the "fixed gulf" that has separated God from sinful man ever since the garden of Eden. (For those who question God's fairness or justice to those who are not His elect from before the beginning of time, this question is addressed in Chapter 12 of this book.)

If, after a person is saved, he or she will study the Scriptures, they can learn about the biblical sequence that God subjected them to in order to accomplish their salvation. Prior to their moment of belief, and even right after that moment, the saved person was unaware of God's ordered activity that brought them to their salvation. As natural men, it was scripturally impossible for them to know it (1 Cor. 2:14).

> 1 Cor. 2:14 But the natural man receiveth not the things of the Spirit of God: for they are foolishness unto him: neither **can** he know them, because they are spiritually discerned.

After salvation, unless a person studies and grows in their knowledge of the Scriptures, they may never realize the extent of God's grace on their behalf. Sadly, many Christians remain uninformed of how they were actually saved. Although, once they are saved, they are forever saved. But sadly, many uninformed believers will spend the remainder of their earthly lives in a state of limited gratefulness for the eternal salvation they were given. How sad. It will be a source of some embarrassment for them at their Bema seat judgment.

(Refer to the appendix of this book for a chart that offers a more detailed explanation of this salvation sequence with Sripture support and the level of involvement of the elect and the non-elect individuals.)

**Election and the Free Will Sequence of Salvation**

Much of the error about this saving sequence has been caused by the fabrication of the doctrine of "free will." Consequently, in this doctrine, they must significantly distort the biblical sequence laid out above. They cannot deny the Biblical fact of election. But they are working from an experiential context. Because they experienced the sensation of choosing to believe, men instinctively take credit for the decision. This belief requires that free will doctrine to make a definitional change to the biblical fact of election to accommodate the place of their free will in their act of belief.

Here is how the chain of events of the free will view of salvation perspective must be altered:

**Election, Made before Time, by God's Foreknowledge of Man's Free Will Choice, Made in Time -> Hearing the Word of God -> Heart Understanding Opened -> Gift of Faith Given -> Man's Free Will Decision to Accept or Reject the Gift -> Belief of the Gospel**

This modification of God's sovereignty in election and the inclusion of their free will prerogative in the belief decision is in direct contradiction to the biblical truth that states "salvation is of the Lord" (Jonah 2:9). Free will doctrine must therefore distort the biblical truth of election by making it contingent upon God's knowing and responding to the choice of man's free will. The typical Arminian (free will) spin of the doctrine of election asserts that God's choice was based on His "foreknowledge" of men's choices about belief. This means that God's predestinating work, as revealed in Ephesians 1:5, done "according to the good pleasure of his will," is only a half-truth, because free will doctrine makes God's choice contingent on man's choice. It implies that the "pleasure" of God's will was to yield to whatever man's free will decided to do.

In the context of salvation, the placement of the will of fallen man over the will of God denigrates any value of being among the elect of God, and it undercuts His sovereignty over salvation. The only place where an act of man's free (unbiased) will caused a change of God's salvific will was in the garden of Eden, when the willful disobedience of Adam (and all men) (Rom. 5:12) occurred. That act was truly a "free will" act of man; a will created by God. Therefore, God's sovereignty cannot be impugned by His response. God responded as He must, with His own standard of justice. "The wages of sin is death." (Rom. 6:23). Unbelief is sin, and sin cannot be tolerated or go unpunished by God.

**The Prime Cause Factor**

Salvation is the result of a string of cause and effect truths that are revealed within the pages of Scripture. Whenever one is investigating or seeking to understand a particular event, it is only natural to seek and determine the underlying or preceding causes that led to the particular event. In our legal system, all matters that are brought to court are analyzed and judged as to the cause of the matter, be it a civil or criminal matter. Creation and life itself are the ultimate issues that drive men to seek the answers to questions like, "Why are we here?" and "How did this (creation) happen?" In the creation question, the issue that is at the fulcrum of the debate is of the "prime cause". Creationists rest upon God's answer of Genesis 1:1. Meanwhile, evolutionists, if they were philosophically honest, should be locked into the answer of "eternal" or "perpetual" evolution. However, the law of causes and effects aren't logically allowed to exist without a prime cause that starts a chain of causes leading to an effect.

Thus, any evolutionist answer I have ever heard always pulls some enormous number of years figure out of the evolutionary hat as being the age of creation—usually in the billions. If they say something like 4.7 billions of years ago creation began, I chuckle and ask why wasn't it 4.8 billion years?

Putting the creation debate aside, it is the point about the prime cause of salvation that this dissertation addresses. Salvation must have a prime cause. That prime cause must be biblically supported, not philosophically or experientially supported. I believe the consensus in Christianity rests upon man's free will as the prime cause of salvation. However, an honest scriptural analysis of this doctrine requires some "hermeneutic creationism" to iron out the scriptural contradictions that free will doctrine creates. Free will theology must twist the truth of God's work of election into a definition that undercuts the depth of this act of grace by God. Natural man naturally hates any such idea of God's election of men. Surprisingly or not, because of their still active sin nature, many Christians want to reject the truth that their sovereign God has chosen and ordained only some men to salvation while passing over others. They persist in creatively using their logic to agree with Satan's original lie of, "Oh God did not really mean or say that." When men attempt to confine God to their ways, they are forgetting Isaiah 55:8-9, which tells them:

> Isa. 55:8 For my thoughts are not your thoughts, neither are your ways my ways, saith the Lord.

> Isa. 55:9 For as the heavens are higher than the earth, so are my ways higher than your ways, and my thoughts than your thoughts.

The truth of election is one of those "ways"!

CHAPTER 10

# Faith - Is It a Gift or a Work?

**Examining Ephesians 2:8–9**

SO, IF MAN'S FREE will is not the spark that activates salvation, then what are the means God uses to enable a person to believe? One of the things many Christians will be surprised to learn in heaven is that the very faith that saved them was His gift to them. I think there is a large segment of Christians today who do not believe this. They could know it now if they would let Scripture speak.

> Eph. 2:8 For by grace are ye <u>saved through faith</u>; and **that** not of yourselves: **it** is the gift of God:

> Eph. 2:9 Not of works, lest any man should boast.

The pronouns (in bold type) in the second portion of verse 8 clarify one of the three subjects mentioned in the first part of verse 8. Note that the pronouns *that* and *it* that are used in the second part of the verse. These pronouns usually get twisted to refer to either "salvation" as the gift and/or "grace" as the gift. Many Bible scholars, who are biased toward free will theology, insist that salvation is the gift referred to. Their common argument is that the gender of the Greek pronouns *that* and *it* do not match the gender of the word *faith*. Therefore, they contend that these pronouns cannot be grammatically connected to the word *faith*. Although this Greek gender translation rule is factual, this particular free will defense fails because of the translation truth about the other two nouns that precede the pronouns *that* and *it*. What the Arminian expositors fail to mention is the gender of the words *salvation* and *grace*.

John Gill (1697–1771) was a theologian and pastor who was followed in his pastorate by Charles Spurgeon. Gill was a staunch defender of the Calvinist position of God's sovereignty in salvation. Gill authored many volumes of commentary on the Bible. Editors later consolidated Gill's works into a multivolume collection titled *John Gill's Exposition of the Entire Bible*. The following commentary contains Gill's exposition of Ephesians 2:8. The first part is what Gill wrote and the second section is a follow-up commentary by the editor who assembled this particular section of Gill's commentary. On the latter part of verse 8, which contain the controversial pronouns that and it, Gill wrote:

> Through faith, and that not of yourselves, it is the gift of God; salvation is through faith, not as a cause or condition of salvation, or as what adds anything to the blessing itself; but it is the way, or means, or instrument, which God has appointed, for the receiving and enjoying it, that so it might appear to be all of grace; and this faith is not the produce of man's free will and power, but it is the free gift of God; and therefore salvation through it is consistent with salvation by grace; since that itself is of grace, lies entirely in receiving grace and gives all the glory to the grace of God: the sense of this last clause may be, that salvation is not of ourselves; it is not of our desiring

nor of our deserving, nor of our performing, but is of the free grace of God: though faith is elsewhere represented as the gift of God, John 6:65.

Then the book editor added this commentary:

(I asked the following question of a Greek and Hebrew professor:

"In this verse, to what does the word "that" refer to? Adam Clarke, Wesley & company say that it is neuter plural and "Faith" is feminine hence it cannot refer to faith, (Such an admission would destroy their theological system.) However "Grace" is also feminine as is "Salvation".

His reply was:

Here you ask a wonderful theological/exegetical question to which I can only give an opinion, and not a definitive answer. The problem is that there is NO precise referent. Grace is feminine. Faith is feminine. And even Salvation (as a noun) is feminine. Yet it must be one of these three at least, and maybe more than one, or all three in conjunction. Since all three come from God and not from man, the latter might seem the more likely. However, it is a tautology [needless repetition of an obvious truth] to say salvation and grace are "not of yourselves," and in that case it certainly looks more like the passage is really pointing out that man cannot even take credit for his own act of faith, but that faith was itself created by God and implanted in us that we might believe (i.e. the normal Calvinistic position). In which regard the whole theological issue of "regeneration preceding faith" comes into play. So, that is basically my opinion, though others obviously disagree strenuously, but from an exegetical standpoint, the other positions have to explain away the matter of the tautology.

(Whether you accept the reply or not, it is sufficient to show that the Greek is not as definitive in this verse as some scholars would have you believe. Editor)[46]

I am not a Greek scholar, but I will accept the answer of the Greek and Hebrew scholar who said that the words *salvation* and *grace* also have a feminine gender.

Scholars will acknowledge that in the Greek language, gender matching between pronouns and their antecedent nouns is a general rule, as opposed to an ironclad rule, in biblical interpretation. Because of the fact that *salvation* and *grace* are also in the feminine gender, the free will defense against faith being a gift from God is discredited. Even if the Greek pronoun *that* is neutral plural and is thus applied to all three nouns, it remains that (saving) "faith" is a gift of God. If a Bible student is not a Greek scholar, then he or she must put a certain degree of reliance on the English to understand what this verse is saying. I would ask that, if it takes knowledge of Greek grammar to rightly divide this important passage, how can "every plowboy in England" (or America, for that matter), ever understand what it says, unless a Greek scholar is available to explain it to him? We must also put reliance upon God's guiding of those who translated the Bible from Hebrew and Greek.

Nevertheless, this verse provides a context. Let the context and grammar of this verse resolve this question. The theme of the first three chapters of Ephesians is salvation. I have no problem agreeing that salvation is the ultimate result of the gift of faith, so in that sense, salvation is surely also a gift. But this passage is revealing a previously unknown truth about the means of salvation—faith. It was not a new revelation for Christ, through Paul, to write that salvation is a gift from God. It was revealed in Romans:

---

46 John Gill, "Ephesians 2:8 Commentary," in *John Gill's Exposition of the Entire Bible,* http://www.biblestudytools.com/commentaries/gills-exposition-of-the-bible/ephesians-2-8.html.

## FAITH - IS IT A GIFT OR A WORK?

> Rom. 6:23 For the wages of sin is death; but <u>the gift of God is eternal life through Jesus Christ our Lord</u>.

Likewise, it was no surprise that grace is also a gift given by God. Paul confirms that grace was given to him by God.

> Rom. 15:15 Nevertheless, brethren, I have written the more boldly unto you in some sort, as putting you in mind, <u>because of the grace that is given to me of God</u>,

Paul also affirms that grace is given to other believers by God.

> 1 Cor. 1:4 I thank my God always on your behalf, for <u>the grace of God which is given you by Jesus Christ</u>.

But the truth that the faith by which we are saved is also a gift of God was a previously unrevealed fact. I firmly believe that the subject of faith, which is cited as the conduit to salvation, is the gift under consideration in Eph. 2:8–9. The phrase "and that not of yourselves" would be an unnecessary amplification if it was applied to the subject of salvation, (a "tautology," as the Greek and Hebrew professor called it). No logical person supposes that salvation was their accomplishment. Likewise, no one believes that grace is "of themselves."

By contrast, faith, however, is commonly believed to be a product of one's own mind and will. This is the core issue that this book argues against. This passage is offered by Paul to correct the common misconception of faith as being a personal accomplishment. Therefore, the phrase, "and that not of yourselves is added as a logical clarifier of the aforementioned subject of faith. It is an essential revelation of a truth that escapes most men.

There are 33 "by faith" verses in Paul's letters alone regarding things that will accrue to believers: i.e., living, the righteousness of Christ, justification, standing, etc. It is the natural response of man's logic to presume that all of these "faith" references are the result of their own self-generated faith. It is a profound revelation to men to be told that the very faith that saved them was a gift from God.

Verse 9 is added to confirm this revelation, where faith is contrasted with works. In many places in his letters, Paul repeatedly emphasizes that it is faith, not works, which brings salvation. Salvation is the ultimate gift that is given through the agency of the gift of faith from God so that "no man can boast." Like it or not, if faith, or even the acceptance of the gift of faith, is an accomplishment of man's "free will," then man does have at least that one accomplishment to boast about in heaven, in contradiction to what verse 9 has just revealed. Nevertheless, most free will proponents oppose this exposition of Eph. 2:8–9.

From the Arminian view, salvation becomes a reward for giving the right answer on a one-question entrance exam. Each individual alone is responsible for choosing the right answer. Those who pass the exam may rightly boast about their answer to this exam, because it was "their" answer.

**Does Everyone Receive the Gift of Faith?**

Free will doctrine must require that every descendant of Adam and Eve be offered the gift of faith that could lead to salvation, if God's fairness is to be maintained. In addition, all men must also be able to understand the offer. Such a scenario defies logic. In contrast, all of mankind, when they were in Adam had the promise of eternal life. They understood God's commands and through their free will in Adam, they failed to believe.

> Rom. 5:12 Wherefore, as by one man sin entered into the world, and death by sin; and so death passed upon all men, for that <u>all have sinned</u>.

If all mankind did not have a part in this "sin decision," then God would be unjust to say "all have sinned" and to pass the judgment of death upon all. Since that sin, saving faith must be given to any who will be saved. But, by God's foreordination, it is only given to His elect, who were chosen for it in eternity past according to the sovereign purpose of His will. Even those who were chosen at this time had no reason or virtue within them to incite God's choice of them. As individuals, we did not know salvation would be given to us, and we can never know who else will receive this gift. We are to be faithful messengers of the offer of salvation and spread this offer to all of the other "whosoevers," because we cannot know who they are.

God can change the heart of the most hardened unbeliever. There is no heart God can't reach. It bears notice of how God opens and changes hearts instantly by His word. Witness the conversions of Paul, Peter and Andrew, James and John:

## Paul

> Acts 9:5 And he said, <u>Who art thou, Lord</u>? And the Lord said, I am Jesus whom thou persecutest: it is hard for thee to kick against the pricks.

> Acts 9:6 And he trembling and astonished said, Lord, <u>what wilt thou have me to do</u>? And the Lord said unto him, Arise, and go into the city, and it shall be told thee what thou must do.

Notice there were no intervening questions between the two underlined questions in these two verses. As soon as Jesus told Paul who He was, Paul knew it and asked for his orders.

## Peter and Andrew

> Matt. 4:18 And Jesus, walking by the sea of Galilee, saw two brethren, <u>Simon called Peter, and Andrew his brother</u>, casting a net into the sea: for they were fishers.

> Matt. 4:19 And <u>he saith unto them, Follow me</u>, and I will make you fishers of men.

> Matt. 4:20 And they **straightway** <u>left their nets, and followed him</u>.

### James and John

> Matt. 4:21 And going on from thence, he saw other two brethren, <u>James the son of Zebedee, and John his brother</u>, in a ship with Zebedee their father, mending their nets; and he called them.

> Matt. 4:22 And <u>they **immediately** left the ship and their father, and followed him</u>.

As soon as Jesus spoke to each of these men, they did not reason, question, or bargain with Him. The two words in boldface emphasize how quickly they obeyed His instructions. They knew internally who had spoken to them, and no further questions ensued. These are clear examples of effectual hearing.

Paul, Peter, Andrew, James and John all responded immediately to the word of God (Jesus).

### "Faith of Jesus" Contrasted with "Faith in Jesus"

I firmly believe that Eph. 2:8–9 is a revelation from Jesus through Paul that tells us it was not even our faith that saved us, but instead it was a gifted faith—the faith <u>of</u> Jesus. Listen to these "faith of" verses:

> Rom. 3:22 Even the righteousness of God which is <u>by faith of Jesus Christ</u> unto all and <u>upon all them that believe</u>: for there is no difference.

> Gal. 2:16 Knowing that a man is not justified by the works of the law, <u>but **by the faith of Jesus Christ**, **even we have**</u>

<u>believed in Jesus Christ</u>, that we might be justified <u>by the faith of Christ</u>, and not by the works of the law: for by the works of the law shall no flesh be justified.

Gal. 2:20 I am crucified with Christ: nevertheless I live; yet not I, but Christ liveth in me: and the life

which I now live in the flesh I live <u>by the faith of the Son of God</u>, who loved me, and gave himself for me.

Gal. 3:22 But the scripture hath concluded all under sin, that the promise <u>by faith of Jesus Christ</u> might be given to <u>them that believe</u>.

Phil. 3:9 And be found in him, not having mine own righteousness, which is of the law, but that which is<u> through the faith of Christ</u>, the righteousness which is of God by faith.

Notice that these verses do not say by "faith in." I realize that the effects of "the faith of Jesus Christ" differ in each of these verses and are not directly stated as the cause of belief. In Rom. 3:22, the effect of the "faith of Jesus" is the righteousness of God; in Gal. 2:20, it is the new life in Christ; in Gal. 3:22, it is the promise; and in Phil. 3:9, again, it is righteousness. But, it must be acknowledged that the effects of these three verses can only exist within the context of being saved.

It could be argued that the phrase "in them who believe," in Rom. 3:22 and Gal.3:22, makes the verb believe the cause of the effects mentioned in each verse. However, the wording of Gal. 2:16 counters that argument. In this verse, by the words I have highlighted in bold print, Paul pointedly reveals that "we have believed" **by** "the faith of Jesus Christ." I suggest that the context of this verse echoes the tone and intent of Ephesians 2:8–9. Both verses reveal that saving faith comes from Jesus Christ. In

Gal. 2:16, we are being told that the "faith of Jesus" is an essential element in any salvation and the resulting benefits it brings.

It is also true that there are several "faith in Christ" verses:

> Gal. 3:26 For ye are all the children of God by <u>faith in</u> Christ Jesus.

> Eph. 1:15 Wherefore I also, after I heard of your <u>faith in</u> the Lord Jesus, and love unto all the saints.

> Col. 1:4 Since we heard of your <u>faith in</u> Christ Jesus, and of the love which ye have to all the saints.

> Col. 2:5 For though I be absent in the flesh, yet am I with you in the spirit, joying and beholding your order, and the stedfastness of your <u>faith in</u> Christ.

Grammatically, these two phrases, "in Christ" and "of Christ," have two different contexts. The former speaks of faith toward Christ, while the latter refers to faith coming from Christ. There is a cause and effect distinction that needs to be made. As Galations 2:16 confirms, the source of our "faith in" Christ is the result of the very gift of the "faith of" Christ. This is the revealed secret given to us in Eph. 2:8–9. It is the "faith of" Christ that precedes and enables our "faith in" Christ. So the "faith" sequence that I find in Scripture occurs in the following order:

1. The "faith of" Christ was demonstrated by: His stepping down into humanity, His life, His death, His burial and resurrection. Atonement made complete.
2. The "gift of faith" was given to the elect according to God's eternal decree made before time and made effective within time (Eph. 2:8–9).

The elect are brought to their salvation by returning the "gift of faith" in the form of their "faith in" Christ—being willfully enabled and responding in belief when they "hear the Word of God" (Rom. 10:17). They will respond with the same immediacy as Paul, Peter, Andrew, James, and John. When God opens a heart to believe, no one resists, however, it is only the hearts of His elect that are opened.

I still hear free will defenders maintain that even after God gives a person understanding by opening his heart to the gospel, that the person can still choose to reject the offer. This assertion is just as absurd. It is analogous to a man on death row receiving a stay of execution on his execution day, being declared not guilty and allowed to walk free, but then refusing both offers in favor of execution. Arminians who assert the possibility of such a refusal of salvation are telling God, "You can't save me if I don't allow it." Furthermore, at the moment of salvation, people are unaware of the gift of faith that they just received. One cannot reject a gift they were unaware of receiving. They can only respond to and apply the gift.

The opening of the heart to understanding leads to belief, by the gift of faith about who Jesus is, all that He has saved them to and saved them from. A rejection of this enlightening would mean that God's heart-opening work failed. A heart-opening is a divine work from God involving the understanding of His Word. Isaiah wrote about the power of the revealed Word of God.

> Isa. 55:11 So shall my word be that goeth forth out of my mouth: <u>it shall not return unto me void, but it shall accomplish that which I please, and it shall prosper in the thing whereto I sent it.</u>

Back to the gift versus work debate, Arminians will consistently deny that the act of faith is a work. Yet they put themselves into a corner, because of their insistence that faith is a personal choice of man alone. But when they are pressed about the gift of Eph. 2:8–9 as being faith instead of salvation or grace, the fallback argument of most Arminians becomes the argument that even if faith is a gift, it must still be accepted by the recipient's free will. This acceptance itself would be a work; ergo the application of saving faith must be affected by a work of man.

**Another Distinction about Faith**

The "faith of Christ" and the "faith in Christ" verses point out a subtle distinction about the topic of faith that requires attention in this sovereignty versus free will debate. Simply put, saving faith is the work of God alone. It is given to whom He wills, and it is given with total effectiveness. It accomplishes its purpose in all of its recipients. People believe because God enables it.

In contrast, once an unbeliever is transformed by the gracious gift of "faith of Christ" leading to salvation, he or she now possesses the seed stock of faith by which the sanctification process, fueled by their "faith in Christ", can now proceed.

> 2 Cor. 9:10 Now he that ministereth seed to the sower both minister bread for your food, and <u>multiply your seed sown, and increase the fruits of your righteousness</u>.

This process advances as the saved individual personally exercises their new faith. They now possess a new nature that factors into the daily sanctification choices they must make. Their will now must fight the daily battle between the draw of their old fleshly (sinful) nature and their new creature nature that is empowered by the indwelling of the Holy Spirit. The will of the believer is clearly confronted with choices to be made under the tension of competing natures.

Why does God allow believers to endure this trial of choices? My answer is for His glory. When acts of faith by believers, such as worship, prayer, witnessing, and giving, are performed by grateful wills, God gets the glory. His gift of saving faith is the source, or "seed," that enables those who are saved to return acts of believing faith, willfully in love. These actions of returned faith are not automatic or robotic. They are choices by the saved person. Any fruitful acts of faith done by believers accrue to God's praise.

> Phil. 1:11 Being <u>filled with the fruits of righteousness, which are **by** Jesus Christ, unto the glory and praise of God.</u>

The fruits of righteousness in believers have their origin in Christ and their accomplishment in the praise of God.

> Eph. 1:6 <u>To the praise of the glory of his grace</u>, wherein he hath made us accepted in the beloved.

> Eph. 1:12 <u>That we should be to the praise of his glory, who first trusted in Christ.</u>

Before concluding this chapter on the role of and truth about the topic of faith, there is another important truth to understand. The "fruits of righteousness" acts of a believer who has been sealed by the Holy Spirit and imbued with the gift of the "faith of Christ," can be outwardly displayed and imitated by persons who have not been transformed by the gift of faith inwardly. The theological term for such people is often "professing Christians."

Such people perform the same acts of Christian worship or service as those who have been saved by the grace of the gift of the "faith of Christ" and who have been sealed with the Holy Spirit. They can, and do, say the same things as true believers. The difference is that their motivation for, and source of, their behavior arises from untransformed hearts. Their motivations often stem from the most common theological lie, which is the belief that some degree of being "good enough" will help secure their salvation. They may say all the right things about Jesus and His atoning death, but in their hearts, they believe that it will be the sum of their "good works," whatever that term encompasses, that will assure their salvation.

The elect who have been saved solely by God's grace should not be surprised or worried by any indistinguishable imitation of "professed believers." Scripture tells us that Satan's abilities of deception are great and that he has always been able to transform himself as light even though he and his ministers are the rulers of darkness.

> 2 Cor. 11:14 And no marvel; for <u>Satan himself is transformed into an angel of light</u>.

> Eph. 6:12 For we wrestle not against flesh and blood, but against principalities, against powers, against <u>the rulers of the darkness of this world</u>, against spiritual wickedness in high places.

This is a distinction that true believers can no more make than the distinction as to whom are the, as yet, unsaved elect of God. Such distinctions are beyond the capacity of true Christians to discern because only God knows and can see what is in the hearts of men. Regardless of the reality of merely professing believers in our midst, it is not our concern, because God will never be mocked or deceived by their false profession or be tricked into saving such people.

> Gal. 6:7 <u>Be not deceived; God is not mocked</u>: for whatsoever a man soweth, that shall he also reap.

> John 10:14 <u>I am the good shepherd, and know my sheep</u>, and am known of mine.

To reiterate the distinction, saving faith is the sole prerogative gift of God, while sanctifying faith is enabled through the indwelling Spirit of Christ and is willfully performed by believers who now are able to make the choice as Joshua stated it:

> Josh. 24:15 And if it seem evil unto you to serve the LORD, <u>choose you this day whom ye will serve</u>; whether the gods which your fathers served that were on the other side of the

flood, or the gods of the Amorites, in whose land ye dwell: but <u>as for me and my house, we will serve the LORD</u>.

These obedience choices are the choices for which all saved persons will stand accountable for at the Bema seat judgment, as stated in 2 Corinthians:

> 2 Cor. 5:10 For we must all appear before the judgment seat of Christ; that every one may receive the <u>things done in his body</u>, according to that he hath done, <u>whether it be good or bad</u>.

"Good and bad" in this verse cannot relate to our sin, because it was paid for at the cross. It can only relate to the return of our "faith in Christ" acts, which can only spring from the gift we received in the "faith of Christ." When the willful acts of service to God and Jesus are made, it is praise to God. The ultimate truth about faith is found in Hebrews.

> Heb. 11:6 <u>But without faith it is impossible to please him</u>: for he that cometh to God must believe that he is, and that he is a rewarder of them that diligently seek him.

The Hebrews 11:6 "pleasing faith" can be none other than the product of the sequential faiths defined above: the "faith of Christ" that produces the "faith in Christ" in God's elect.

CHAPTER 11

# God's Sovereignty in Salvation

THE FOLLOWING ARE THREE arguments offered to support the sovereignty position. The misuses of these points, by those who champion free will doctrine, are pointed out, as well as the correct biblical context of them in the salvation event.

**Argument 1: Opened Hearts**

If a man could see, hear, and understand in his heart, apart from God causing it to happen, why does God need to open a heart as He did for Lydia? Scripture tells us about the heart-opening work of God that He provided for Lydia in Acts 16:14. In the interest of "free will" fairness and doctrinal consistency, it is only fitting that this same work of "opening" must be provided to everyone before their decision to believe or reject is made. Arminians might concede to God's determination of the timing of anyone's heart opening, but I do not see how they can deny the fact that the same heart revelation that Lydia received, must, in fairness, be made to all men. Whenever and however such an opening happens, according to free will theology, the belief decision, made by each person, is based upon the evidence presented to them. Free will advocates would say that this decision is totally reserved to, and dependent upon, the individual's will and nothing more. Nevertheless, for God to be just to all who have a free will, all must receive the same "heart-opening fair chance" to independently respond to the evidence.

It must then be asked, what is it in a man that causes him to accept or reject the gospel? As shown previously, the Bible confirms that all men are inherently aware of God's existence. But this spiritual salvation decision must go beyond the awareness of God, as revealed in Romans 1:19–20. James tells us that even the demons know God and tremble with fear. But demons were not made in God's image, and they have no savior offered to them. Men, however, are required by God, at some point in their life, to fear and obey the God to whom all creation testifies. Solomon confirms this at the end of Ecclesiastes.

> Eccl. 12:13 Let us hear the conclusion of the whole matter: Fear God, and keep his commandments: for <u>this is the whole duty of man</u>.

From the Arminian view, by whatever means God uses, all men must be made aware of their spiritually fatal sin condition and of God's offer of salvation through the work of His Son, Jesus Christ. In the eyes of free will doctrine, if there was even one man who was never aware of sin and of the atoning work of Christ, it would discredit God's attribute of His justice. Ignorance (or unawareness) would become a valid excuse for avoiding responsibility for such a man. Free will doctrine must concede that the truth of sin and salvation must be presented and revealed to every man's heart, thereby giving every person a free will chance to decide, for God to be fair and for all men to be held accountable.

In the Arminian formula, whatever is revealed to the "opened" heart must be sent to the mind for a "free will" decision. Does God ever intercede in the hearts and minds of men? The Psalms alone contain 121 references to the heart and God's interaction with it. It is very strange that God, throughout the Bible, frequently intervenes, not only in the understanding of men, but also in the hearts of men to guide His ordained course of human events. Yet, to maintain pure free will doctrine, the crucial salvation decision must be made purely on the basis of some level of mental awareness, comprehension, and intellect of the individual. This decision cannot possibly be left to the realm of dumb luck. However, any deeper involvement of God in salvation is prohibited by free will doctrine. The implicit fairness principle of Arminianism cannot deny it.

**Argument 2: The Decision Process**

Again, why or how is each man's decision to believe, or refuse to believe, made? It is a question that demands a free will (Arminian) answer. It is a question that poses a problem for the free will (Arminian) position. Given the doctrinal supposition that this momentous verdict about God's offer of salvation is made totally within the jury room of each person's mind, God must abstain fairly and justly from any meddling or compulsion in the decision process. Man is left to weigh whatever evidence has been presented to him. He must use whatever degree of intellect and understanding he has to make the most important decision of his life about God's offer of salvation.

It is a fact that our lives consist of a constant stream of decisions. Decisions are not made in a vacuum. Decisions are effects that must have at least one cause. Decisions are made in response to at least one, if not many, influences (causes). They may be internal, physical motivations, like hunger, pain, or just an itch. Motivations for a decision often have an external component. Man's physical senses and his emotions are often the receptors of these influences, and they, in turn, become the determiners of each decision based on the options available. There are also instinctive reactions, like jerking one's hand away from a flame. These are involuntary moves that involve no conscious thought process. However, it is the decision process that involves conscious, voluntary choice-making that needs further consideration.

We usually make such conscious choice decisions based upon our personal preferences that are derived from our acquired experiences and/or knowledge. For example, suppose you are out to dinner at an all-you-can-eat buffet restaurant. If the buffet offers a food item that, on previous occasion, has made you sick or that you are allergic to, you will not take a helping of that food. On the other hand, you may see a certain food that is one of your favorites. You may take a generous helping, but you will not overload your plate with it because you know (or should know) your own eating capacity. The law of diminishing return, plus the fact that you know that too much of any food can also make you sick, will limit your intake of even your most favorite food item. So you (hopefully) exercise prudence in the amount of this favorite food you take. Prior personal experience and knowledge guide your food selections.

The point I wish to make about the free will doctrine that dictates a man's decision about salvation, is that it must be a choice, by definition, free from any compelling or will-altering influence from God. It must be a choice motivated by some intellectual ability or perceptiveness within the individual. Free will doctrine makes certain implications about such a momentous decision that, by default, are implausible in any application to all men.

### Responsibility Requires Comprehension

How? First of all, it must be acknowledged that not every human has had, or now has, access to a Bible or to biblical teaching. But, though it may be possible for God, it strains credibility to believe that He appears to all remaining mankind, who never have any sort of access to the Bible, to give them a mandatory, clear moment of comprehension of their need for salvation. But they must get a sufficient degree of understanding to give them a fair, free will chance to make this eternal decision. If God did not sovereignly choose men to salvation before the beginning of time by His own will, as the Arminian argument asserts, then all men must have some opportunity, at some point in their lifetime, to intellectually make this salvation decision, in order to be held accountable by God.

But, there are millions of people who have passed, or will pass, through their lives having never heard about Jesus, let alone given any thought about Him. Consider a person who is born, lives his or her whole life, and dies in the jungles of the Amazon, the Artic region of the Eskimos, the ghettos of Bangladesh, or the nomadic sands of the Sahara. You cannot deny that some, if not many, people in any one of these locales, could pass a whole lifetime without hearing anything about Jesus Christ. They have an innate knowledge of God (Rom. 1:19-20), through the witness of His creation, which makes them "without excuse" about the existence of a creator God. Nevertheless, they will die with no knowledge about Jesus, yet they will still stand inexcusable before God. Is this fair of God? Rom. 9:14-15 answers this question with a truth that does not just apply to Israel alone:

> Rom 9:14 What shall we say then? <u>Is there unrighteousness with God? God forbid.</u>

Rom 9:15 For he saith to Moses, <u>I will have mercy on whom I will have mercy, and I will have compassion on whom I will have compassion.</u>

Dr. Vance and Arminians twist this passage and will usually argue that it deals with the choosing of the nation Israel by God, while not choosing other nations as His elect. They maintain that election has nothing to do with individual salvation. It is curious why Arminians argue against God having the same prerogative of mercy or of hardening a heart regarding individual salvation as He does with His choice of extending mercy to His chosen nation. They allow corporate election but not personal election. Their argument deflates when Paul assigns this term to individuals. The apostle Paul was called to minister to the Gentiles. The term Gentiles does not denote a nation, but rather individuals who are not Jewish. Yet the following four verses are examples of Paul writing to and calling various individuals "elect."

Rom. 8:33 Who shall lay any thing to the charge of God's elect? It is God that justifieth.

Col. 3:12 Put on therefore, as <u>the elect of God</u>, holy and beloved, bowels of mercies, kindness, humbleness of mind, meekness, longsuffering.

2 Tim. 2:10 Therefore I endure all things for <u>the elect's sakes</u>, that they may also obtain the salvation which is in Christ Jesus with eternal glory.

Titus 1:1 Paul, a servant of God, and an apostle of Jesus Christ, according to the faith of <u>God's elect</u>, and the acknowledging of the truth which is after godliness.

There is no view of Israel or any nation involved in these applications of the term elect. Paul was writing to Gentile believers. Consider the following verse in John's gospel. The Greek for the word *chosen* is from the same root word as the word elect in the previous verses. Jesus is plainly telling his disciples that He was the one who did the choosing of them.

> John 15:16 <u>Ye have not chosen me, but I have chosen you, and ordained you</u>, that ye should go and bring forth fruit, and that your fruit should remain: that whatsoever ye shall ask of the Father in my name, he may give it you.

As Dr. Vance is glad to point out, this specific choosing of Jesus relates to the appointed ministry of the twelve. If Jesus does not retain sovereignty in all of His "electing" (choosing), it makes one wonder why Jesus makes the point about His choice of them and not their choice of Him. Dr. Vance scoffs at the frequent application of Calvinism to the subject of salvation, but if the twelve disciples' salvation was the result of their "free will" choice, then Jesus cannot correctly say it was not their choice that brought them to their apostolic position and assignment. Nevertheless, in John 15:16, Jesus makes the specific point about who chose whom.

**Where and How the Belief Decision Is Made?**

The second unsustainable implication of free will doctrine is the assumption that God does communicate the gospel truth to everyone by applying the fourth process of "heart hearing" to at least one of the other 3 hearing methods mentioned—by hearing, by reading or by a direct dream or vision. The change wrought in their heart by the Holy Spirit leads to their final decision in their mind because the mind is where such decision-making information gets processed and choices are made. The mind will choose what the heart desires.

Allowing, for argument's sake, that absent God's sovereign choosing, every man must therefore get some sort of heart opening, à la Lydia (Acts 16). As pointed out earlier, whatever is opened to one's heart must be sent to the mind for the decision to be made. I have heard a free will advocate teach that this is what is meant when Scripture says Lydia "attended to the things spoken." This free will advocate taught that Lydia thought about Paul's message and responded positively. Remember, the other women heard the same message, but the Scripture says nothing about their response. What about the hearts of the other women? If Lydia made her "free will" decision because of the opening of her heart, as this passage suggests, how is it fair to the other women, whose hearts, we can reasonably presume, were not opened? If their hearts were opened, it is curious why only Lydia's free will came to the choice to believe. The free will of the others turned down the same message that Lydia accepted. Perhaps she was just that much more perceptive than her fellow worshippers. All we know from this account in Acts 16 is that Lydia got something the other women did not. If she decided "to believe" apart from any spiritual influence, according to the Arminian (free will) view of salvation, then it seems to me that Lydia will have a boast in heaven, because she attended to what she heard, while the other women did not.

Why does the mind become critical in the free will formula? Because it must contend that the opening of Lydia's heart, at most, only gave her something to think about. This is how free will advocates must diminish the phenomena of the "opening" of a heart by God. It is factual that the Bible abounds with God's workings within the hearts of men. But curiously, in the salvation transaction, according to free will doctrine, God willingly restrains himself from exerting any influence over the choice beyond a heart revelation. So the only free will option left is to conclude that the final evaluation of the salvation offer must happen in a mind, that is free from any influence of God.

What about the heart? Remember, in theology, the heart of man is used as a metaphor for the part of man that both separates him from and connects him to God. Scripture has much to say about the heart of fallen man that is not a flattering picture:

> Gen. 8:21 And the Lord smelled a sweet savour; and the Lord said in his heart, I will not again curse the ground any more for man's sake; for <u>the imagination of man's heart is evil from his youth</u>; neither will I again smite any more every thing living, as I have done.

> Eccl. 9:3 This is an evil among all things that are done under the sun, that there is one event unto all: yea, also <u>the heart of the sons of men is full of evil, and madness is in their heart while they live, and after that they go to the dead.</u>

> Jer. 17:9 <u>The heart is deceitful above all things, and desperately wicked</u>: who can know it?

(These three verses are very explicit depictions of the condition of man's heart. They are obviously not the hearts that God created in Adam and Eve.)

> Ezek. 36:26 <u>A new heart also will I give you</u>, and a new spirit will I put within you: and <u>I will take away the stony heart out of your flesh, and I will give you an heart of flesh.</u>

(Here is the prophecy about what God will, as yet, do for Israel's heart. If it was not evil [fleshly], then a new heart would be unnecessary.)

> Mark 7:21 For from within, <u>out of the heart of men, proceed evil thoughts, adulteries, fornications, murders,</u>

> Mark 7:22 <u>Thefts, covetousness, wickedness, deceit, lasciviousness, an evil eye, blasphemy, pride, foolishness:</u>

> Mark 7:23 <u>All these evil things come from within, and defile the man.</u>

(This is a teaching from Jesus, who knows what the hearts of fallen men produce.)

Luke 6:45 A good man <u>out of the good treasure of his heart</u> bringeth forth that which is good; and an evil man out of the evil treasure of his heart bringeth forth that which is evil: for of the abundance of the heart his mouth speaketh.

(This is another teaching of Jesus that confirms the role that the heart plays in the actions that men produce. You must think about what makes any man good or evil in God's eyes.)

Yet, I can hear some who would argue that mankind is still able to make a "free will" heart choice to believe the gospel. Let's see if Scripture confirms this. Scripture affirms that understanding does happen in the heart, but if one thinks that the understanding needed to make the correct "free will" choice to believe comes from within their own heart, listen to what the following list of verses about the noun "understanding" and the verb "understand." If one thinks that God (Jesus) plays no part in what men do and do not understand, please note the underlined words in the verses below:

Luke 24:45 <u>Then opened he their understanding</u>, that they might understand the scriptures,

Rom. 1:18, 31 Men, who hold the truth in unrighteousness [are],,, <u>without understanding</u>, covenantbreakers, without natural affection, implacable, unmerciful.

1 Cor. 1:19 For it is written, I will destroy the wisdom of the wise, and <u>will bring to nothing the understanding of the prudent</u>.

Eph. 1:18 <u>The eyes of your understanding being enlightened</u>; that ye may know what is the hope of his calling, and what the riches of the glory of his inheritance in the saints,

Eph. 4:18 <u>Having the understanding darkened</u>, being alienated from the life of God through the ignorance that is in them, <u>because of the **blindness of their heart**</u>.

2 Tim. 2:7 Consider what I say; and <u>the Lord give thee understanding in all things</u>.

1 John 5:20 And we know that the Son of God is come, and <u>hath given us an understanding</u>, that we may know him that is true, and we are in him that is true, even in his Son Jesus Christ. This is the true God, and eternal life.

Matt. 13:14 And in them is <u>fulfilled the prophecy of Esaias</u>, which saith, By hearing <u>ye shall</u> hear, and <u>shall not understand</u>; and seeing ye shall see, and shall not perceive:

Matt. 13:15 For this people's heart is waxed gross, and their ears are dull of hearing, and their eyes they have closed; <u>lest at any time they</u> should see with their eyes, and hear with their ears, and **should understand with their heart**, and should be converted, and I should heal them.

Luke 8:10 And he said, Unto you it is given to know the mysteries of the kingdom of God: but to others in parables; <u>that</u> seeing they might not see, and hearing <u>they might not understand</u>.

John 8:43 <u>Why do ye not understand</u> my speech? even because ye cannot hear my word.

John 12:40 He hath blinded their eyes, and **<u>hardened their heart</u>**; that <u>**they should not**</u> see with their eyes, nor **<u>understand with their heart</u>**, and be converted, and I should heal them.

Acts 28:27 For **the heart of this people is waxed gross**, and their ears are dull of hearing, and their eyes have they closed; lest they should see with their eyes, and hear with their ears, and understand with their heart, and should be converted, and I should heal them.

Note specifically in Eph. 4:18, Matt. 13:15, John 12:40, and Acts 28:27 that, the point is plainly made that God purposely blocks man's heart understanding, which, in turn, could cause a free will decision to believe and force God to save them. Remember the earlier point about how men's will makes all choices based upon the strongest desire or motivation within them at the moment of decision. This is the irresistible part in God's miracle of salvation. When God opens the hearts of His foreordained, "whomsoever He wills", a new understanding is given and is responded to by a new enlightened desire of the will. Were it otherwise, this heart opening act of a sovereign God could be stymied by the will of a man who is beyond the realm of God's sovereign control.

The verses above make it quite evident that the Lord both opens and darkens man's understanding of the truth of salvation, as He wills. The reason for this activity is repeatedly stated above in Matt.13:15, John 12:40, Acts 28:27, all of which are references to a prophecy of Isaiah:

Isa. 6:10 Make the heart of this people fat, and make their ears heavy, and shut their eyes; lest they see with their eyes, and hear with their ears, and understand with their heart, and convert, and be healed.

(This verse certainly sounds like an intrusion by God upon any supposed "free will" of man.)

Man makes decisions all his life based upon mental processes, but the understanding required for genuine salvation must happen the heart. Again, Romans 10 says it with certainty and clarity.

Rom. 10:9 That if thou shalt confess with thy mouth the Lord Jesus, and shalt **believe in thine heart that** God hath raised him from the dead, thou shalt be saved.

It is only God that can provide such enlightened understanding that leads to "heart belief".

Eph. 1:17 That the God of our Lord Jesus Christ, the Father of glory, may give unto you the spirit of wisdom and revelation in the knowledge of him:

Eph. 1:18 The eyes of your understanding being enlightened; that ye may know what is the hope of his calling, and what the riches of the glory of his inheritance in the saints,

In these verses, Paul was not praying that his readers would be "enlightened" by the reasoning abilities of their respective free wills.

**Argument 3: Fallen Man in God's Eyes**

How can fallen man believe in his heart? There is no amount of spin that can be applied to these verses that can erase the truth that God will not let man acquire any credit or glory for his own ability to see, hear, or understand his helplessness and thereby choose salvation. Mankind, bound in sin since their fall in Adam, can never become deserving of salvation by their own, unassisted belief. Scripture does not provide an encouraging picture of mankind's spiritual condition. Read these underlined descriptors of lost men.

2 Tim. 2:26 And that they may recover themselves out of the snare of the devil, who are taken captive by him at his will.

Luke 4:18 The Spirit of the Lord is upon me, because he hath anointed me to preach the gospel to the poor; he hath sent me to heal the brokenhearted, to preach deliverance to the captives, and recovering of sight to the blind, to set at liberty them that are bruised.

Rom. 5:10 For if, when we were enemies, we were reconciled to God by the death of his Son, much more, being reconciled, we shall be saved by his life.

Col. 1:21 And you, that were sometime alienated and enemies in your mind by wicked works, yet now hath he reconciled.

James 4:4 Ye adulterers and adulteresses, know ye not that the friendship of the world is enmity with God? whosoever therefore will be a friend of the world is the enemy of God.

Rom. 8:21 Because the creature itself also shall be delivered from the bondage of corruption into the glorious liberty of the children of God.

Gal. 4:3 Even so we, when we were children, were in bondage under the elements of the world.

Heb. 2:15 And deliver them who through fear of death were all their lifetime subject to bondage.

2 Pet. 2:19 While they promise them liberty, they themselves are the servants of corruption: for of whom a man is overcome, of the same is he brought in bondage.

Eph. 2:1 And you hath he quickened, who were dead in trespasses and sins.

Eph. 2:5 Even when we were dead in sins, hath quickened us together with Christ, (by grace ye are saved.)

Col. 2:13 And you, <u>being dead in your sins and the uncircumcision of your flesh,</u> hath he quickened together with him, having forgiven you all trespasses.

Now ask yourself, how can a person logically, by a free will choice, decide to walk away from being a captive, from being an enemy, from being in bondage, and, in the ultimate truth, from being dead in their sins? Apart from Jesus, there has never been a person since the fall, who does not come under all of these descriptions. Consider, again, the truth of this sequence of verses.

Rom. 3:23 <u>For all have sinned,</u> and come short of the glory of God.

"All" means all. Jesus tells us about the fate of anyone who sins.

John 8:34 Jesus answered them, Verily, verily, I say unto you, Whosoever committeth sin is the servant of sin.

Next, the last part of 2 Peter 2:19 tells me that those who have become "servants of sin" are in a servitude that has overcome them and thereby put them "in bondage."

2 Pet. 2:19 While they promise them liberty, they themselves are the servants of corruption: <u>for of whom a man is overcome, of the same is he brought in bondage</u>.

Free will advocates sincerely want to believe that they can simply escape, or walk away from, their "captivity," their servitude, their bondage, and their "enemy" status, by their own willful decision. I believe Scripture contradicts any such ability of man. They treat the call of Scripture and the wooing activity of the Holy Spirit, like a salesman on their doorstep, making his sales pitch and anxiously awaiting their choice. Fallen men are deemed in Scripture as spiritually dead. To be resurrected from this state of death, a "spirit quickening" is needed. Dead men, physically or spiritually, cannot simply decide to be quickened.

Recalling Dr. Vance's proposition that while a man can be held accountable for his unwillingness to obey, but not for his inability to obey, the answer to this dilemma is simple. Man's fallen nature is Satan's captive. The source captivity was man's unwillingness, in Adam, to believe. Thus, the inability to believe, that Dr. Vance cannot allow, is simply the result of man's choice to be unwilling to believe; the very condition that Dr. Vance concedes makes a man accountable. Man's falling into an inability to believe is the nature he acquired by the very free will nature originally endowed to him by his Creator. Man moved himself from the state of being responsible and able, into the state of inability by falling into bondage to Satan.

Men can no more disregard and overcome the restraints of their fallen spiritual nature than they can exceed the limits of their physical nature. Man, in Adam, was created with the free will opportunity to obey or disobey that fairness demands of God's justice. But, when "all sinned in Adam" (Rom. 5:12), the will of man was taken captive by Satan.

> Rom. 6:16 Know ye not, that to whom ye yield yourselves servants to obey, his servants ye are to whom ye obey; whether of sin unto death, or of obedience unto righteousness?

And compounding their predicament, they were deceived by sin and Satan with the lie that let them believe that now they were their own gods. (Gen. 3:5)

> Gen. 3:5 For God doth know that in the day ye eat thereof, then your eyes shall be opened, and ye shall be as gods, knowing good and evil.

The degree of man's lost predicament is a truth revealed in 2 Cor. 4:4:

## GOD'S SOVEREIGNTY IN SALVATION

> 2 Cor. 4:4 In whom <u>the god of this world hath blinded the minds of them which believe not</u>, lest the light of the glorious gospel of Christ, who is the image of God, should shine unto them.

So not only is man dependent upon God's will for understanding, but he held in blindness by the ruler of this world, Satan. What power does a man's will have to overcome the ruler of this world, Satan, and willfully escape their blindness? What power does a man's will have to overcome these two supernatural truths about understanding and blindness?

The two previous verses are two biblical truths that testify to the fact of the inability of the individual to escape the captivity that was created by his own free will act, in Adam. The whole purpose of Scripture is to show men: 1. because of their sin, they need a Savior, 2. how God provided the Savior, 3. how they must receive the Savior, and 4. how they are to glorify God. The next verse below tells us, how and when the salvation sequence was initiated.

> 2 Tim. 1:9 Who hath <u>saved us</u>, and called us with an holy calling, not according to our works, but <u>according to his own purpose and grace</u>, which was <u>given us in Christ Jesus before the world began</u>.

How did God provide salvation? *According to his own purpose and grace.*
Where was that salvation to be found? *Given us in Christ Jesus.*
When was this salvation determined? *Before the world began,*

### Total Sovereignty or Relinquished Sovereignty?

It is a biblical fact that through the history of His creation, God has allowed some actions to occur that, while they were not beyond his control, they were allowed to be in direct opposition to Him. God allowed Lucifer, the highest of all the angels, to covet and rebel against His exalted position of authority. He allowed

Satan the freedom to tempt Eve in the Garden. He allowed Adam and Eve the freedom to willfully choose to disobey and forfeit their eternal life and relationship with Him. He allows Satan to have temporary dominion over this present creation and over all men from the moment Adam sinned. In short, God allowed evil to arise and operate within His creation. However, the most significant truth about all of these allowed, negative facts is that, in God's eternal plan, they were all overcome by the death, burial, and resurrection of His Son, according to His eternal plan and purpose.

But it is not true that God can or will ever allow man to initiate the salvation process and regain his salvation by the exercise of a will that, as free will proponents persistently maintain, must remain free from any influence or compulsion of God. Why? Two reasons: First, as just stated, it would mean that there was a part of His creation that would continue to exist beyond the cross that would never be, by definition, under His sovereign control. God could never bring this age and creation to an end because there would never cease to be a free will person who has, as yet, not received his or her "fair" opportunity to choose. Even to say it was His choice to allow it would mean that His sovereignty would be made less than complete—a contradiction of logic. How could God leave this eternally crucial decision in any degree of control of lost men, who are plainly called His enemies? Relinquished control means relinquished sovereignty.

> Rom. 5:10 For if, when <u>we were enemies</u>, we were reconciled to God by the death of his Son, much more, being reconciled, we shall be saved by his life.

> Col. 1:21 And <u>you, that were sometime alienated and enemies in your mind</u> by wicked works, yet now hath he reconciled.

The other reason that refutes the theory of man's free will to believe is that, if it is a continued reality, then Jesus cannot correctly be called the author and finisher of our faith (Heb. 12:2). It would be each man's free will faith that saved him and, thereby, each man would be the true "author" of his own salvation.

> Heb. 12:2 Looking unto Jesus <u>the author and finisher of our faith</u>; who for the joy that was set before him endured the cross, despising the shame, and is set down at the right hand of the throne of God.

In free will doctrine, Jesus is demoted to being an insurance salesman at your door, selling eternal life policies that can't go into effect until you decide to sign up for it. At the very least, free will doctrine must picture salvation as being co-authored by the Lord and each individual who chooses to "freely" believe; "freely" being necessarily defined as apart from God's working or compulsion. Scripture, however, says no such thing. This is a violation of His sovereignty that God cannot allow. God can never be less than sovereign.

CHAPTER 12

# Additional Arguments Against Free Will Doctrine

**Is God Fair?**
THE DOCTRINE THAT MAKES predestination of the elect by God the prime cause of every salvation ignites an Arminian explosion of accusations against God of being unfair, of being the author of sin, of being a hypocritical Savior who offers salvation to all with no intent that all may receive it (and that's just to name a few). A popular accusation is the one that accuses God of "double predestination." But, to be accurate, in the larger picture of God's ways, there can only be either double predestination or no predestination at all. Single predestination if it was true, would make predestination of no unique honor to man. It would become like a belly button; we would all have the same destination.

Arminians logically assert that the passing over of some for salvation by God is in fact a predestining of them to condemnation. However, there is a distinct difference between the elect's predestination to salvation and the non-elect's destination for eternal punishment. The elect's destination is God's choice, while the non-elect's destination was the consequence of their own willful choice. All of the elect will know that their salvation was purely by the grace of God. Arminians may believe that the double predestination argument is an irrefutable point that defeats the doctrine of election as Calvinism defines it, but they overlook the truth of whose decision initiates each destination.

Unfortunately, the predestinating work of God, as it is revealed in Scripture, is a subject of theology where human logic often persists in overriding God's sovereignty over His creation. It is where men instinctively pass judgement on what God would not, or could not, do. They view and define Scripture according to their logic and fail to see it from God's perspective. God undoubtedly blessed man with faculty of logic, to be used as part of how he understands God and the world around him. However, a truth revealed in God's Word reminds us that the logic of even saved men is still subject to their old nature. The reality of man's fallibility means that any truth in the Bible is always vulnerable to being erroneously bent to conform to human logic. Nonetheless, our sovereign God is not bound to conform to man's logic in all He does, as Daniel tells us,

> Dan. 4:35 And all the inhabitants of the earth are reputed as nothing: and <u>he</u> (the Most High—verse 34) <u>doeth according to his will in the army of heaven, and among the inhabitants of the earth</u>: and <u>none can stay his hand</u>, or say unto him, What doest thou?

Scripture also confirms God's right to choose. Read Jer. 18:6 and Rom. 9:21:

## ADDITIONAL ARGUMENTS AGAINST FREE WILL DOCTRINE

Jer. 18:6 O house of Israel, cannot I do with you as this potter? saith the Lord. Behold, <u>as the clay is in the potter's hand, so are ye in mine hand, O house of Israel</u>.

Rom. 9:21 <u>Hath not the potter power over the clay, of the same lump to make one vessel unto honour, and another unto dishonour</u>?

The prophecy of Isaiah must be repeated,

Isa. 55:8 <u>For my thoughts are not your thoughts, neither are your ways my ways, saith the Lord</u>.

Isa. 55:9 For as the heavens are higher than the earth, <u>so are my ways higher than your ways, and my thoughts than your thoughts</u>.

The truths of the previous verses are unfortunately neglected or overlooked by free will theology when the topic of predestination arises. God's attribute of His justice, in the free will mind, is violated by any act of predestinating of men to salvation. It is an understandable reaction when viewed from and with man's logic.

However, taking a deeper look at the creation and fall of Adam, God is acquitted of the charge of injustice for His predestinating of men. When Adam was created, he was perfect in God's eyes. Adam was not created to die. The only reason for death is sin. Sin was the free choice that God allowed Adam to make. Theoretically, had he not sinned, all of Adam's posterity would likewise never die. Added to that, theoretically, is the fact that if Adam had not sinned, his eternal state would, in some small measure, have to be credited to his own continued, willful obedience alone. Adam could never be correctly labeled as having been saved because there would never be anything to be saved from. God would not get the glory. Rom. 11:36 would be negated. In fact, the whole Bible would be nonexistent because man (Adam) would already have a perfect, personal relationship with God.

> Rom. 11:36 <u>For of him, and through him, and to him, are all things: to whom be glory for ever</u>. Amen.

**Four Options Regarding Fallen Man**

When Adam sinned, God had 3 theoretically possible options. First, He could have saved all men from the penalty of death, physical and spiritual. We know from Scripture that this will not happen. The Scriptures offer ample detail about the punishment for sin. There is an eternal punishment in hell first and then in the lake of fire for all unbelievers. The Bible is not lacking in references about hell. If universal salvation was God's purpose, then the biblical warnings about hell would be unnecessary, if not disingenuous. In the book of Revelation we are told that at the judgment seat of Christ, Satan, his angels, and unbelievers from all ages will be cast into the lake of fire, forever. The word *forever* is frightening. Think about this. Even the worst judgments issued from man's justice system—whether the death penalty or life imprisonment—have an end to them. The words *eternal* and *forever* mean what they mean. Words like *probation* or *parole* and man-fabricated doctrines like *purgatory* have no biblical foundation or connection to the promise of eternal punishment in hell.

The second option is that God could have chosen to save no one after "all died in Adam." Likewise, the Bible does not support this possibility. If this was true, Christ simply would have had no reason to come to earth and die for sin.

The third remaining option is that God could have saved all of those whom he chose before the foundation of time according to the purpose of His will, while leaving the remainder of men dead and condemned in their choice that they made, when they were in Adam. This is the option chosen as the Scriptures tell us:

# ADDITIONAL ARGUMENTS AGAINST FREE WILL DOCTRINE

> Eph. 1:4 <u>According as he hath chosen us in him before the foundation of the world</u>, that we should be holy and without blame before him in love.

> Eph. 1:5 Having predestinated us unto the adoption of children by Jesus Christ to himself, <u>according to the good pleasure of his will</u>.

> 2 Tim. 2:19 Nevertheless the foundation of God standeth sure, having this seal, <u>The Lord knoweth them that are his</u>. And, Let every one that nameth the name of Christ depart from iniquity.

> 2 Tim. 2:20 <u>But in a great house there are not only vessels of gold and of silver, but also of wood and of earth; and some to honour, and some to dishonour</u>.

> John 17:2 As thou hast given him power over all flesh, that he should <u>give eternal life to as many as thou hast given him</u>.

Although Scripture clearly denies the exercise of options one and two (as refuted by these verses in Eph. and 2 Tim.), the point to be acknowledged here is that none of these three options violate God's attribute of justice. He would have been absolutely fair in the exercise of any of these three options.

However, free will (Arminian) theology proposes a fourth option that replaces all three options above. They maintain that God will save all men who decide, by their free will, to believe the gospel. This belief is built upon two points. First, is the biblical fact of God's attributes of eternal omniscience. God is all knowing and exists outside space and time, which confines mankind. Second, they misapply the verse of Romans 8, which says:

Rom. 8:29 <u>For whom he did foreknow, he also did predestinate</u> to be conformed to the image of his Son, that he might be the firstborn among many brethren.

This verse is the source of a creative interpretation used to prove the free will doctrine that asserts that God "foreknew" who would believe. This is another oft-repeated heresy of free will doctrine. By His foreknowledge of men's action of belief, God could predestine all whom He knew would believe. It escapes their notice that the verse emphasizes the foreknowing particular persons ("For <u>whom</u> he did foreknow."). If the free will interpretation was true, Rom. 8:29 should read, "For whom would believe he did foreknow." However, Scripture says nothing about God's knowledge of man's choice as the determinant of His predestinating choice.

This fourth, alternate option of free will theology simply violates the sovereign will of God. There is an unacceptable implication to it. If this option were true and as argued above, it would mean that God created and allowed something to exist in His creation that has, and will, remain forever outside His sovereign rule. It is illogical to assert that a sovereign God can create and allow anything that will always remain beyond His sovereign control. If man's will remains free, as free will doctrine asserts, then the best God can do is to be a pleader and beggar to men with His offer of salvation. It means that the same God spoken of in Isa 55:8 ("For my thoughts are not your thoughts, neither are your ways my ways, saith the LORD.") must rely totally on the hope that men might yield to His pleadings. This is inconceivable.

Consider all that God has done to reveal salvation to man, such as His creation of man, His choice of Abram, His choosing of and formation of the nation of Israel, His promise of and deliverance of a Savior through the Law and the Prophets, His display of grace through the earthly life of Jesus (Christ's death,

## ADDITIONAL ARGUMENTS AGAINST FREE WILL DOCTRINE

burial and resurrection), and His ultimate revelation of the mysteries of the gospel of grace through the apostle Paul. In spite of all these works of God, free-will doctrine still maintains that man retains control of the ultimate first cause of salvation: his free will choice to believe. It is as if man can say to God, "I may see all you have done, but I'll get back to you with my decision."

To those who question God's fairness in His predestinated choice of some, but not all to salvation, the answer will be made clear to everyone in eternity. Indulging in purely personal speculations, I believe that every unsaved person who enters to an eternity in hell, will do so with the full knowledge that they were aware of God and that they, in some manner, personally rejected Him. If nothing else, I have to believe that all such persons will know that they participated with Adam's choice to disobey God and then chose to remain in that choice. If they even think of protesting, lost men will be confronted by God, who says,

> Rom. 9:20 Nay but, O man, <u>who art thou that repliest against God</u>? Shall the thing formed say to him that formed it, Why hast thou made me thus?

At their judgment, lost men will make a confession that would have saved them, but now is the truth that condemns them:

> Phil. 2:10 That at the name of Jesus every knee should bow, of things in heaven, and things in earth, and things under the earth.

Lost men will be aware that the truth of God's sovereign choice not to save them was based on their choice to not believe Him through their entire lives, including the moment of their free will choice of sin in Adam. If nothing else, what they will know is that it was their own sin that condemned them, as Zanchius wrote[47]. The reader may disagree with the point of these speculations, but they are offered in light of the biblical

---

47 Zanchius, 74–75.

fact that all condemned men will have no complaint or defense to offer before their judge. God will never be judged or accused by lost mankind for His sovereign choices. As Romans puts it,

> Rom. 1:20 For the invisible things of him from the creation of the world are clearly seen, being <u>understood by the things that are made</u>, even his eternal power and Godhead; <u>so that they are without excuse.</u>

> Rom. 3:19 That <u>every mouth may be stopped</u>, and all the world may become guilty before God.

Conversely, every saved man will know that they were also guilty before God, but that their choice to believe in the gospel was initiated and enabled by God's choice in eternity past to save them and by the power of the Holy Spirit that worked in their hearts. But the greatest revelation to them will be the fact that their salvation was totally by His grace alone. There was no reason that originated within them that caused God to choose them. The following verses confirm that any personal boasting is impossible and that man's knowledge of all truth in heaven will be illuminated:

> Rom. 3:27 <u>Where is boasting then? It is excluded</u>. By what law? of works? Nay: but <u>by the law of faith.</u>(It was by <u>the faith of Christ</u>. If it was by their own free will faith they would have a boast.)

> Eph. 2:9 <u>Not of works, lest any man should boast.</u>

> 1 Cor. 13:12 For now we see through a glass, darkly; but then face to face: now I know in part; but <u>then shall I know even as also I am known.</u>

A difference in the eternities between the unbeliever and the believer will be this: An unbeliever will know that his unbelief was his personal choice and was the cause of his eternal condemnation. He will know his guilt without protest and with eternal remorse. By contrast, the believer will know that he was a guilty unbeliever who was redeemed from his guilt by the total grace of the blood and resurrection of Jesus Christ, and the sovereign election to salvation by God the Father, made before the beginning of creation. He will have no boast about his salvation and will be eternally grateful to God alone for salvation.

Like Jonah, all believers will know and confess, "Salvation is of the Lord"(Jonah 2:9).

CHAPTER 13

# Contexts, New Signage, Food for Thought, Last Words

**Contexts to Remember**

HERE IS A LIST of some biblical principles and a sequence of facts about man and his salvation that I offer as a contextual overview of the relationship between God's sovereignty and man's free will, as I perceive them from Scripture:

> Acts 15:18 Known unto God are all his works from the beginning of the world.

1. God did not and cannot create anything that is not "good."
2. Nothing occurs in eternity that is outside God's purpose and sovereign will.
3. God cannot learn anything He does not already eternally know.

4. God created the angels with a free will to obey or disobey Him—before creation and the beginning of time.
5. God allowed Lucifer, the highest of the created angels, to use his free will, rebel against Him, and become the father of lies and all evil—before creation and the beginning of time. This was purposed (point 2) by God.
6. God allowed a third of the angelic host to join Lucifer in his rebellion—before creation and the foundation of time.
7. God chose certain people of all mankind to be saved—before creation and the beginning of time.
8. God did not choose the remainder of all mankind to be saved—before creation and the beginning of time.
9. The people that comprise the two groups of points 7 and 8 above were, and are, eternally known only to the mind of God. However, God has told men of the existence of each group by His sovereign act of choice or non-choice.
10. God created this present creation, including all mankind, in Adam, in six literal days—approximately 4,000 BC.
11. God's creation, including all of mankind, was made to be an eternal creation. Death did not exist.
12. God created Adam and Eve with the same free will to obey or disobey that Satan and the angels possessed.
13. Unlike any of the angels, Adam (man) was created in the image of God.
14. The angels differ from man in that they were not made in the image of God, nor did God ever provide any Savior or path of salvation for the angels who fell into sin.
15. God allowed Satan an unimpeded opportunity to tempt Adam and Eve (and all men) into disobedience of God's commands.
16. God allowed Adam, Eve under Adam's authority, and all of Adam's posterity (in Adam) to use their free will to either obey or disobey Him in the Garden.

17. Thus, all men, who were in Adam at his creation, possessed, at that time, a will that can be truly called free.
18. Because of the truth of point 16, every man is born responsible for his sin in Adam.
19. Adam's choice to disobey was counted (imputed) by God as the choice of all mankind.
20. God put mankind and all creation under His announced curse for their sin.
21. The free wills of Satan, his angels, and mankind became powerless to revoke their respective curses of God. Neither Satan, nor mankind, can use their own wills to choose to restore their relationship with God as He created it.
22. Both Satan and mankind now have wills that guide their actions to do what they want to do, by now being their own gods.
23. Satan's successful temptation of Adam and Eve in the Garden resulted in the dominion of the earth passing from man to Satan.
24. All of Adam's descendants are born into a state of natural enmity toward God and in bondage to Satan.
25. Mankind, made in the image of God, having God's laws written in his heart, can, and does, willfully and occasionally obey these laws, but without the possibility that the sum of his own willful obedience can ever restore his eternal state with God. By no deeds of the flesh can any man be saved.
26. Just as the Godhead took steps to prevent man from physically re-entering the Garden and partaking of the Tree of Life to gain eternal life by his own actions, so also has God denied man, by any willful act of his own, the power to believe to eternal life. It is the result of the curse of a spiritual separation that man alone cannot choose to be saved.

27. By His mysterious way, God still commanded men, in the Garden of Eden, in His chosen nation Israel, during Christ's earthly ministry and in the dispensation of grace, to willfully obey and believe whatever gospel was given to them at their respective times in history, even though He sovereignly knew of their fallen inability to personally do so.
28. As eternally determined, God, in due time, provided the way of salvation by the life, death and resurrection of His Son, Jesus Christ.
29. In further due time, God revealed the only access to this salvation was by faith and the offer of salvation by faith was laid open to all men.
30. God, in still further due time, revealed the mystery through Paul that the faith required for salvation cannot be accomplished by man alone, but instead it is a gift from Him, given only to all whom He chose to salvation before the foundation of time. (point 7. above)
31. God purposed that His predestined (elect) men would be the communicators of His gospel of salvation to other lost men.
32. All those who are saved, in turn, are to share the gospel of the grace of Jesus Christ with all mankind, because only God has the foreknowledge of who are the elect or non-elect to salvation.
33. Some truths about God's salvific will that most of Christendom fails to comprehend.
    a. No man knows who God's predestined choices for salvation are, thus their faithful spreading the gospel to all men, without knowing who God has chosen, glorifies Him.
    b. God uses His word, whether written, preached, or spoken directly by Him through dreams and visions, coupled with the regenerating power of the Holy

Spirit, to activate the faith that enables the choice by the predestined man to believe and be saved. The elect must be spiritually enabled to believe.

c. God leaves the non-chosen (non-elect) men, with a closed heart, to continue in their original sin in Adam and to continue to rebel against Him by rejecting to believe both the general call and, in some cases, the specific gospel call of God.

d. Lost men will die in their pride believing that at any time of their life, they could have believed God by their own wills but chose not to.

34. God's justice will be perfectly executed when He condemns the non-elect, who willfully, in Adam, chose to sin against Him, to an eternal punishment in the lake of fire. They will have no excuse for their own sin, nor will they have any accusation to bring against God for their non-election.

35. God's grace will be fully revealed when His elect are ushered into their eternal inheritance, having no boast of their own for their salvation, specifically excluding any "free will" act of their own. They will, then, fully know that the scope of grace that saved them was completely undeserved.

36. Who God chose for salvation and why He chose them is not ours to know, except what we do know is that God is love and the fullness of His grace will be shown by His act of sovereign election of men. It is rooted in His love. The way God used to redeem all elect people brings all glory to Him for His grace.

## New Signage for the Gateway into Heaven

Remember, in the introduction of this book, the commonly drawn picture of the gateway to heaven that so many pastors use to portray man's will and God's sovereignty as an incomprehensible mystery? Let me redraw this scene for you. I would alter the signage on the outside approach to this blessed gate that many say reads:

"Whosoever will"

I would alter that phrase to read, "Whomsoever I will"

Under this phrase I would add any or all of the verses below:

> Acts 13:48 And <u>when the Gentiles heard this</u>, they were glad, and glorified the word of the Lord: and <u>as many as were ordained to eternal life believed.</u>

> Phil. 1:29 For <u>unto you it is given</u> in the behalf of Christ, not only <u>to believe on him</u>, but also to suffer for his sake.

> Rom. 9:15 For he saith to Moses, I will have mercy <u>on whom I will</u> have mercy, and I will have compassion <u>on whom I will</u> have compassion.

> Rom. 9:16 So then it is <u>not of him that willeth, nor of him that runneth</u>, but of God that sheweth mercy.

On the inside of this gate, I would leave the phrase commonly used which reads, "chosen in Him before the foundation of the world."

Under this phrase I would add Paul's beautiful doxology of Romans 11,

> Rom. 11:33 O the depth of the riches both of the wisdom and knowledge of God! how unsearchable are his judgments, and his ways past finding out!

> Rom. 11:34 For who hath known the mind of the Lord? or who hath been his counsellor?

> Rom. 11:35 Or who hath first given to him, and it shall be recompensed unto him again?

> Rom. 11:36 For of him, and through him, and to him, are all things: to whom be glory for ever. Amen.

These modifications to the signage of this hypothetical gate would leave no room for doubt by men that they were saved completely by the grace of God.

The only mystery that every believer will be left with is the thought borrowed from David's expression of awe about God's concern for man. David wrote:

> Ps. 8:4 What is man, that thou art mindful of him? and the son of man, that thou visitest him?

As believers pass through this hypothetical gate and enter heaven, they will marvel in a manner similar to David in Ps. 8:4.

They will forever wonder and praise God saying, "Who was I that you, God, were mindful of me?"

**Some Final Food for Thought**

Before I conclude my defense of God's sovereignty, here is a final tidbit to either challenge or affirm your view of this issue, depending upon your position.

Most mature Christians will agree that the commonly repeated adage of, "God helps those who help themselves," is unscriptural. But is that not exactly what the doctrine of free will implies? Despite all that God has done to provide for man's salvation, God cannot help man until man decides to help himself by believing the gospel. Only then, according to the Arminian view, can God quicken and save man. The free will doctrine insistence that God knew this before the beginning of time is irrelevant in light of the fact that His saving work remained contingent upon man's willful act of belief. God's knowing all things is not as significant as the fact of His causing of all things. If God just knew something that He did not cause, then He is not sovereign.

**Last words**

It is my hope that the preceding citation of numerous scriptures, the exposition applied to those scriptures and the logical conclusions presented, may help in some way to clarify, or change, the reader's understanding of how the two realities of God's predestinating sovereignty and man's willful choice to believe, are incorporated into a non-contradictory theology of salvation. These two realities of scripture are not as mysterious as many theologians are inclined to conclude.

The logic and scriptural exposition I have applied is, of course, finite and fallible. It is a fact, almost every verse I referenced has been used and exposited to a different end by Dr. Vance in his treatise against the sovereignty position. We both used, or divided if you will, scripture to build and support our respective doctrinal positions. But, the fact remains that, of these two respective positions in the debate about the first cause of salvation, only one can be true. I conclude my defense with these thoughts. I have referenced several books that deal with this eternal issue of God's sovereignty in salvation in relation to man's will in salvation. I have shared the views of several prominent writers along with my own opinions, pro and con, about their positions. The truths of God's sovereignty and man, at one time having a free will, cannot be denied. Nevertheless, these two biblical truths cannot be blended into an equally causative role in the doctrine of salvation, despite many clever philosophical attempts to do so. Salvation cannot have two prime causes. This is doctrinal stand-off that demands an answer.

To those who insist on the necessity of the free will of man in salvation, my answer to that stand-off is condensed in the title I gave this book. "99% Grace?". By this title, I am pointing to the major flaw of the doctrine of free will. God has predetermined everything that has happened, is happening, and will happen in His creation. This predetermination, much to the angst of many Christians, includes both who will be, and who will not be, saved, without detracting one iota from His justice or from man's responsibility for his sin. By using the Arminian (free will) explanation of how salvation occurs, no one can ever rationally give God 100% glory (credit) for anyone's salvation. If the free will doctrine were true, then, by any logic, at the least, 1% of the credit for salvation must remain with the individual for his free will choice. Yet, all glory for salvation can only belong to God. All of these nuggets of Scripture and logic are offered as parting thoughts to challenge the idea that God is anything less than sovereign in salvation. This includes the His acts of foreordaining salvation on whoever he chooses, according to nothing other than His good will.

The resolution of this debate does not depend upon any skillfulness of my defense of it, or upon volume of arguments that Dr. Vance and the other "free will" theologians may generate. Every Christian must ultimately rely upon the Holy Spirit within him, who "will guide you into all truth" (John 16:13); who will guide you to the truth about how anyone is saved.

If, after you have read this defense of God's sovereignty in salvation and the criticism of the error of the free will doctrine of salvation, you might be tempted to throw up your hands and utter the Hillary Clinton-esque response of, "What difference does it make?" It is my hope that this presentation of this most important Bible question will help the reader to seek, think about, and find, the correct answer; the answer that gives all of the glory, belonging to God, for your salvation. This is what difference it makes. May God get all glory from you for your salvation; not just 99%.

As for me and my salvation I say, "To God be the glory, great things He (and He alone) hath done." 100% grace! What do you say?

# Postscript

From this lengthy defense of God's sovereignty in salvation, I make no insinuations about the salvation of anyone who holds to the free will view of salvation. This debate does not concern what a person truly believes in their heart, because only God knows the contents of any heart. My concern is what is believed about the process of how the Lord gives salvation. The importance I attach to this debate is the giving to God the glory and praise due Him for the gift of salvation. I fear that all born again believers who enter through heaven's gate with the sincere belief that their free will played a necessary role in their salvation will experience some of the shame that is mentioned in 2 Timothy 2:15, when they stand before the Lord at the Bema seat.

> 2 Tim. 2:15 Study to shew thyself approved unto God, a workman that <u>needeth not to be ashamed</u>, rightly dividing the word of truth.

Any doctrine held that depreciates the total glory belonging to God will be a cause of embarrassment to the believer. For all false (professing only) Christians or unbelievers, any erroneous doctrine they believe will not be their problem. They will never stand before the Bema seat. At the Great White Throne judgment their unbelief is the only matter that will be of eternal consequence to them.

Having the biblically correct understanding of how God saves anyone should increase one's gratitude for their own salvation and equip them to counter the false premises and accusations of free will doctrine. The ultimate truth regarding salvation, drawn from the whole of the Bible is this:

God must receive 100 percent glory for every salvation.

Every saved man can only receive 0 percent glory for his eternal salvation.

Every lost man will bear 100 percent guilt for his eternal condemnation in hell.

# Appendix

## 1. Sequence of Salvation (S.O.S. Chart)

| Salvation Sequence | Scriptural Support | Man's Involvement |
|---|---|---|
| #1. Election of individuals To Salvation by the Will of God before creation. | Eph 1:4-5<br>John 1:12-13 | None |
| #2. A Hearing of The Word of God | Romans 10:17 | For the Elect - it is required. For the Non-Elect - it is possible, but uneffective.* |
| #3. A Heart Opened To Understand what was Heard of the Word of God | Acts 16:14 | Unaware - The Elect will receive it. Unaware - Non-Elect do not receive it. |
| #4. The Gift of Faith Given by Grace of God | Ephesians 2:8-9 | Unaware - The Elect will receive it. Unaware - Non-Elect do not receive it. |
| #5. The Gospel is Believed Because of the effects of Sequences 1, 2, 3, and 4 | Romans 10:9-10 | The Elect willfully enabled - believe. The Non-Elect with unenabled, fallen wills - refuse to believe. |

| #6. Salvation Granted Because of the gift of the Faith of Christ being willfully returned as the Faith in Christ** | 2 Thess 2:13<br>Gal 2:16 | The Elect are now saved because of God's grace and His applied Salvation Sequence. The Non-Elect remain in their willful unbelief. |

\* All men, "in Adam", had their first hearing of God's Word in the Garden of Eden, which led to their responsibility for their fall into sin. Prior to salvation, as yet unsaved elect men must have a subsequent hearing of the Word of God to proceed with their salvation sequence. All fallen, non-elect men may or may not have a subsequent hearing of the Word of God, but any hearing will have no effect on their hardened hearts and blinded understanding.

\*\*Gal. 2:16 "...by the faith of Jesus Christ, even we have believed in Jesus Christ...."

## 2. Definition of Deus Ex Machina
### (From: literarydevices.net)

*(Author's comments are in italics)*

The term deus ex machina refers to the circumstance where an implausible concept or a divine character is introduced into a storyline, for the purpose of resolving its conflict and procuring an interesting outcome.

*(The Biblical conflict being resolved is how salvation is initiated - by God's will or man's will.)*

## APPENDIX

The use of deus ex machina is discouraged, for the reason that the presence of it within a plot is viewed as a sign of an ill-structured plot.

*(This opinion given in the context of fictional writings of men, of which the Bible is not. It is a God written and God resolved plot.)*

Requirements of Deus Ex Machina

Deus ex machinas are solutions. They are not to be seen as unexpected twists and turns in the storyline that end up making things worse, and not as something that contributes towards changing the understanding of the story. Further, it must be shown that the problem solved by a deus ex machina is one that is unsolvable or otherwise hopeless.

*(Salvation by the will of man, apart from God's will, is the hopeless problem solved by a deus ex machina. John 15:5 defines man's helplessness – Eph. 2:8 solves it.)*

It is also that they are sudden or unexpected. This means that the inherent capacity of deus ex machina to solve the mystery is not apparent until the time the device is actually employed to procure a viable ending for the plot.

*(In Scripture, the apparency of God's interventions in the salvation process are sudden, done according to His will (Eph. 1:5). They are also perpetual. Their existence was unknown to men until the clear revelation of them in Eph. 2:8.)* *(The dilemma is solved.)*

However, if some other type of intervention – like common sense – could have been employed to procure the same result, then no matter how sudden the solution is, it would not be termed as deus ex machina.

*(This is essentially the very grounds by which free will doctrine dismisses the profound truth of election by God of men to salvation. They credit the faculty of man's will as the determinant of salvation and thus as the solution to the dilemma.)*

# Scripture Index

**Scripture Index – from KJV**

| Verses | page(s) |
|---|---|
| Gen. 1:26-31 | 92,93 |
| Gen. 2:16-17 | 45,96,97 |
| Gen. 3:5 | 19,39,40,80,123,196 |
| Gen. 3:7-11 | 98,125,126 |
| Gen. 3:22-23 | 125 |
| Gen 6:5 | 31,100,104 |
| Gen. 8:21 | 189 |
| Exo. 20:5 | 95 |
| Deut. 29:4 | 126 |
| Deut. 29:29 | 18,153 |
| Josh. 1:8 | 123 |
| Josh. 24:15 | 178 |
| 1 Sam. 13:14 | 71 |
| 1 Chr. 16:13 | 156 |

| Verse(s) | page(s) |
|---|---|
| Psa. 3:8 | 156 |
| Psa. 8:4 | 217 |
| Psa. 14:2-3 | 124 |
| Psa. 49:12 | 47 |
| Psa. 50:21 | 16 |
| Psa. 51:5 | 98 |
| Psa. 121:4 | 21 |
| Prov. 3:5 | 23 |
| Prov. 16:18 | 22 |
| Eccl. 7:29 | 46 |
| Eccl. 9:3 | 189 |
| Eccl. 12:13-14 | 85, 182 |
| Isa. 6:10 | 192 |
| Isa. 48:8 | 144 |
| Isa. 55:8 | 15, 73, 153, 164, 203, 206 |
| Isa. 55:9 | 16, 164, 203 |
| Isa. 55:11 | 175 |
| Isa. 65:2 | 144 |
| Jer. 8:5 | 143 |
| Jer. 10:23-24 | 144 |
| Jer. 13:23 | 78, 144 |
| Jer. 17:9 | 189 |

## SCRIPTURE INDEX

| Verse(s) | page(s) |
|---|---|
| Jer. 18:6 | 203 |
| Lam. 3:26 | 74,75 |
| Ezek. 36:26 | 189 |
| Dan. 4:35 | 156,202 |
| Jonah 2:9 | 162,209 |
| Matt. 4:18-20 | 171,172 |
| Matt. 4:21-22 | 172 |
| Matt. 7:11 | 98 |
| Matt. 8:12 | 114 |
| Matt. 13:14-15 | 191 |
| Matt. 19:25 | 35 |
| Matt. 22:13 | 115 |
| Matt. 22:14 | 130 |
| Matt. 22:37 | 79 |
| Matt. 24:51 | 115 |
| Matt. 25:30 | 115 |
| Matt. 26:41 | 78 |
| Matt. 27:51-52 | 119 |
| Mark 7:21-23 | 189 |
| Mark 9:23-24 | 80,81 |
| Mark 9:44 | 121 |
| Luke 2:25 | 73 |

| Verse(s) | page(s) |
|---|---|
| Luke 2:36-38 | 74,75 |
| Luke 4:18 | 193 |
| Luke 6:45 | 190 |
| Luke 8:10 | 191 |
| Luke 8:12 | 71 |
| Luke 8:15 | 71 |
| Luke 13:28 | 115 |
| Luke 16:22-26 | 113,114 |
| Luke 19:12-14 | 124,125 |
| Luke 19:14 | 32 |
| Luke 24:45 | 128,160,190 |
| John 1:6-7 | 128 |
| John 1:12-13 | 105,157,223 |
| John 2:25 | 69 |
| John 3:16 | 86,139 |
| John 5:28-29 | 117,121 |
| John 6:28-29 | 67 |
| John 6:39 | 58 |
| John 6:44 | 157 |
| John 6:65 | 69,157,167 |
| John 8:34 | 195 |
| John 8:36 | 132 |

## SCRIPTURE INDEX

| Verse(s) | page(s) |
|---|---|
| John 8:43 | 69,191 |
| John 8:44 | 32 |
| John 10:14 | 178 |
| John 10:28 | 58 |
| John 12:39-40 | 72,191 |
| John 15:5 | 47,79,148 |
| John 15:16 | 187 |
| John 15:23 | 31 |
| John 16:13 | 17,219 |
| John 17:2 | 205 |
| Acts 9:5-6 | 171 |
| Acts 13:48 | 216 |
| Acts 15:18 | 211 |
| Acts 16:14 | 128,160,181,223 |
| Acts 16:30-31 | 66 |
| Acts 17:10-11 | 16 |
| Acts 23:9 | 22 |
| Acts 28:27 | 70,126,127,192 |
| Rom. 1:3-4 | 118 |
| Rom. 1:18 | 190 |
| Rom. 1:19-20 | 82,83,129,182,208 |
| Rom. 1:21-24 | 42 |

| Verse(s) | page(s) |
|---|---|
| Rom. 1:31 | 190 |
| Rom. 2:8-9 | 42 |
| Rom. 2:11-15 | 82 |
| Rom. 2:14 | 32 |
| Rom. 2:15 | 82 |
| Rom. 3:19 | 208 |
| Rom. 3:20 | 46,99 |
| Rom. 3:22 | 172 |
| Rom. 3:23 | 96,195 |
| Rom. 3:27 | 208 |
| Rom. 3:28 | 124 |
| Rom. 5:6 | 59 |
| Rom. 5:10 | 31,194,198 |
| Rom. 5:12 | 89,111,120,163,170 |
| Rom. 5:18 | 60 |
| Rom. 6:16 | 98,111,196 |
| Rom. 6:23 | 33,97,163,169 |
| Rom. 7:6 | 112 |
| Rom. 7:7 | 23,80 |
| Rom. 7:21-25 | 23,104,105 |
| Rom. 8:10-11 | 118 |
| Rom. 8:14 | 131,157 |

## SCRIPTURE INDEX

| Verse(s) | page(s) |
|---|---|
| Rom. 8:21 | 194 |
| Rom. 8:29 | 135,206 |
| Rom. 8:33 | 186 |
| Rom. 9:8 | 32,155 |
| Rom. 9:11 | 154,156 |
| Rom. 9:14-16 | 185,216 |
| Rom. 9:18-20 | 23,24,148,207 |
| Rom. 9:21 | 203 |
| Rom. 9:22-23 | 152,153 |
| Rom. 10:9 | 86,192,223 |
| Rom. 10:17 | 86,160,175,223 |
| Rom. 11:33 | 132 |
| Rom. 11:33-36 | 216,217 |
| Rom. 11:36 | 204 |
| Rom. 14:7-9 | 84 |
| Rom. 15:15 | 169 |
| 1 Cor. 1:4 | 169 |
| 1 Cor. 1:19 | 190 |
| 1 Cor. 1:26 | 130 |
| 1 Cor. 2:14 | 34,100,124,161 |
| 1 Cor. 13:12 | 208 |
| 1 Cor. 14:33 | 11,18 |

| Verse(s) | page(s) |
|---|---|
| 1 Cor. 15:3-4 | 159 |
| 1 Cor. 15:21-22 | 33,89,111,131 |
| 1 Cor. 15:23 | 118,119 |
| 1 Cor. 15:39 | 82 |
| 1 Cor. 15:54-56 | 106 |
| 2 Cor. 4:3-4 | 31,126,127,129,197 |
| 2 Cor. 5:6-8 | 116 |
| 2 Cor. 5:10 | 179 |
| 2 Cor. 5:14 | 122 |
| 2 Cor. 5:17 | 104 |
| 2 Cor. 5:18 | 110 |
| 2 Cor. 9:10 | 176 |
| 2 Cor. 11:14 | 178 |
| Gal. 2:16 | 172,224 |
| Gal. 2:20 | 173 |
| Gal. 2:21 | 124 |
| Gal. 3:22 | 173 |
| Gal. 3:26 | 174 |
| Gal. 4:3 | 194 |
| Gal. 5:18 | 157 |
| Gal. 6:7 | 178 |
| Eph. 1:3-6 | 149,150 |

## SCRIPTURE INDEX

| Verse(s) | page(s) |
|---|---|
| Eph. 1:4 | 9,12,160,205,223 |
| Eph. 1:5 | 9,135,160,162, 205,223 |
| Eph. 1:6 | 177 |
| Eph. 1:11 | 9,13,135 |
| Eph. 1:12 | 177 |
| Eph. 1:13 | 155 |
| Eph. 1:15 | 174 |
| Eph. 1:17 | 193 |
| Eph. 1:18 | 128,130,190,193 |
| Eph. 2:1 | 112,148,194 |
| Eph. 2:2 | 32,111 |
| Eph. 2:3 | 32,148 |
| Eph. 2:5 | 112,120,194 |
| Eph. 2:6 | 112 |
| Eph. 2:8 | 68,81,149,160,165,169,170,172,174,175,225 |
| Eph. 2:9 | 68,81,160, 165,170,172,174,175,208,225 |
| Eph. 3:2 | 66,104 |
| Eph. 4:8-9 | 115 |
| Eph. 4:18 | 128,191 |
| Eph. 6:12 | 178 |
| Php. 1:11 | 177 |
| Php. 1:29 | 130,216 |

| Verse(s) | page(s) |
|---|---|
| Php. 2:10 | 207 |
| Php. 3:9 | 173 |
| Php. 3:18 | 31 |
| Col. 1:4 | 174 |
| Col. 1:21 | 31,194,198 |
| Col. 2:5 | 174 |
| Col. 2:12 | 112 |
| Col. 2:13 | 112,195 |
| Col. 3:12 | 186 |
| 1 Thess. 4:16-17 | 120 |
| 2 Thess. 2:12 | 42 |
| 2 Thess. 2:13 | 136,224 |
| 2 Tim. 1:9 | 149,150,197 |
| 2 Tim. 2:7 | 191 |
| 2 Tim. 2:10 | 186 |
| 2 Tim. 2:15 | 8,27,221 |
| 2 Tim. 2:19-20 | 205 |
| 2 Tim. 2:26 | 193 |
| 2 Tim. 3:16 | 22 |
| 2 Tim. 4:18 | 58 |
| Tit. 1:1 | 186 |
| Tit. 2:11 | 128 |

## SCRIPTURE INDEX

| Verse(s) | page(s) |
|---|---|
| Tit. 3:5 | 155,158 |
| Heb. 2:15 | 194 |
| Heb. 4:15 | 94 |
| Heb. 9:27 | 111 |
| Heb. 11:6 | 154,179 |
| Heb. 12:2 | 199 |
| James 2:10 | 123 |
| James 4:1 | 23 |
| James 4:2 | 23 |
| James 4:4 | 31,194 |
| 1 Pet. 1:20 | 135 |
| 1 Pet. 3:15 | 4 |
| 1 Pet. 4:6 | 116 |
| 2 Pet. 2:19 | 194,195 |
| 1 John 3:23 | 66 |
| 1 John 4:1 | 17 |
| 1 John 5:20 | 191 |
| Rev. 20:4-6 | 119 |
| Rev. 20:11-12 | 116,117,118 |
| Rev. 20:14-15 | 121 |

Below is a lyrical account of the author's transformation from his helpless bondage to sin and Satan, to his eternal freedom in Christ, by the riches of the grace God through His predestined choice.
(lyrics to be sung to the tune of the hymn, "Just As I Am", as written in 1835 by Charlotte Elliott)

### "Justas Iam, My Will and Me"

1. "Justas Iam, my will and me,
always believing my will was free,
The gospel, it called me, e'er Jesus to choose,
But 'twas mine alone to believe or refuse.

2. Justas Iam, my will and me,
how Jesus had saved me, I failed to see.
Thinking by my will, the choice was all mine,
Ne'er did I know t'was God's plan divine.

3. Justas Iam, my will and me,
now by God's grace He set me free.
A captive of Satan, my will was impaled,
I would not choose, but God's choice prevailed.

4. Justas Iam, my will and me,
elect of God, He let me see.
Had He ne'er chosen by His sovereign will.
by my choice alone, I would be dead still.

5. Justas Iam, my will and me,
I could not hear, I could not see,
Then He opened my heart to hear His Word,
by His gift of faith, my salvation occurred.

6. Justas Iam, my will and me,
now this is why I have no plea.
By the grace of God I did succumb,
O lamb of God, I come, I come.

www.ingramcontent.com/pod-product-compliance
Lightning Source LLC
Chambersburg PA
CBHW061636040426
42446CB00010B/1447